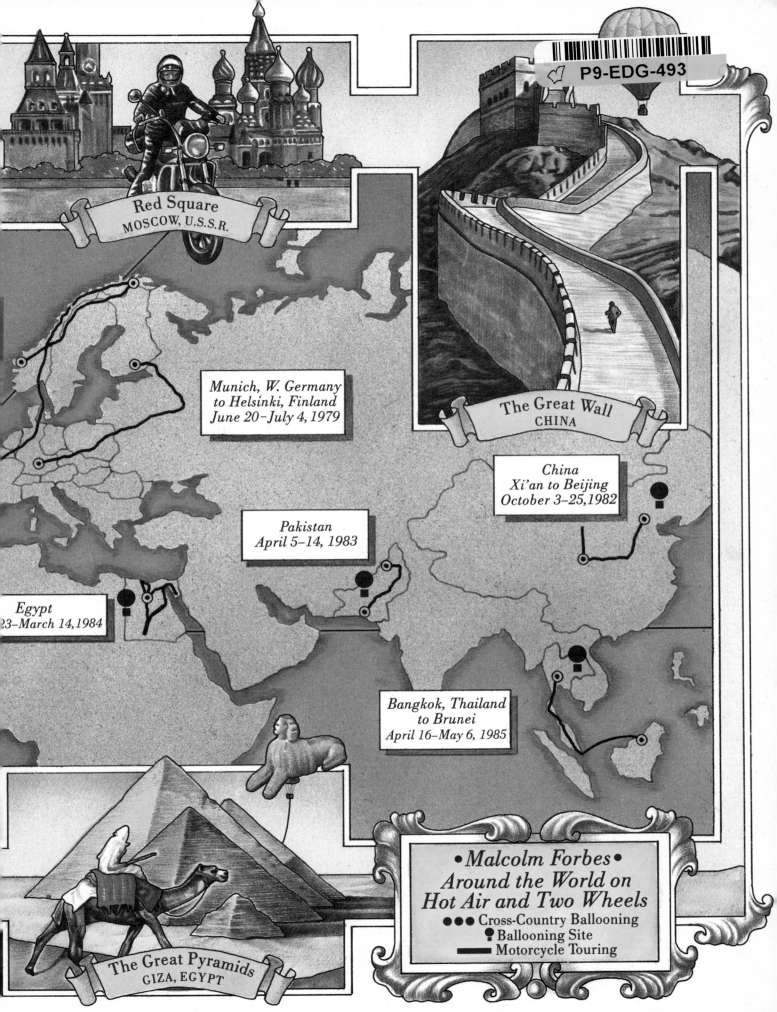

P9-EDG-493

Red Square
MOSCOW, U.S.S.R.

The Great Wall
CHINA

Munich, W. Germany
to Helsinki, Finland
June 20–July 4, 1979

China
Xi'an to Beijing
October 3–25, 1982

Pakistan
April 5–14, 1983

Egypt
23–March 14, 1984

Bangkok, Thailand
to Brunei
April 16–May 6, 1985

The Great Pyramids
GIZA, EGYPT

•Malcolm Forbes•
Around the World on
Hot Air and Two Wheels
●●● Cross-Country Ballooning
🎈 Ballooning Site
▬ Motorcycle Touring

FORBES MAGAZINE HAILS
EGYPTIAN - U.S. AMITY

Malcolm Forbes

AROUND THE WORLD ON HOT AIR & TWO WHEELS

SIMON AND SCHUSTER

New York

LIBRARY OF CONGRESS CATALOGING IN PUBLICATION DATA
FORBES, MALCOLM S.
    AROUND THE WORLD ON HOT AIR & TWO WHEELS.
    1. FORBES, MALCOLM S.   2. VOYAGES AND TRAVELS—1951–   .   3. BALLOON
ASCENSIONS.   4. MOTORCYCLING.
I. TITLE.
G465.F65   1985   910.4   85-2456
ISBN: 0-671-60031-1

Grateful acknowledgment is made to the following publications for permission to reprint these articles:

"Introduction: Why?"—*Playboy* magazine, April 1, 1979.
"A Frenchman Meets the Capitalist Tools"—*Moto-Journal*, July 26, 1984.
"America from Coast to Coast"—*National Aeronautics* magazine, April–June 1974.
"Ballooning the Atlantic"—*Ballooning* magazine, Spring 1975.
"London/Normandy/Morocco"—*Cycle* magazine, January 1979.

"On the Road to Moscow"—*Road Rider* magazine, October–November 1979.
"In the Land of the Midnight Run"—*Cycle World* magazine, December 1980.
"Pakistan"—FORBES magazine, June 20, 1983.
"Egypt"—*Cycle* magazine, March 1985.
"The Elephant Has Landed"—FORBES magazine, July 29, 1985.

Page 262. "On the Road Again," words and music by Willie Nelson. © 1979 Willie Nelson Music, Inc. All rights reserved. Used by permission.

Contents

Foreword

FARAWAY PLACES invariably fascinate everyone but the people living in them. For us, as you will see in these chapters by our fellow travelers, cycling through the Russian countryside or a Chinese village or a crowded Pakistani port was exciting. But to those there, of course, almost anywhere else would probably be more so.

All of us, when we acquire a wee bit more than the bare necessities of life, want to begin living. To adventure outside our accustomed cocoons is what the wings of mind and legs of body are for.

Sure, the adventures in this book, with their less conventional ways of wandering, involve getting to some parts of the globe not easily accessible for reasons political or economic. But that's not the point. These pages simply suggest that daydreams *are* doable. The turn-on is not in scale, spectacle, or cost. It's in the doing.

Anything you haven't done is an adventure. Wanting to is the principal requirement. If you can do and want to, don't not.

Those of us involved in the trips chronicled here hope you'll enjoy sharing them. We hope that if you have a yen—and some bucks—you'll be moved to stir your stumps, to get up and go.

In short, while alive, live.

Malcolm Forbes

Introduction:

"People think you're eccentric if you ride a motorcycle. Unless you're poor. If you're poor they think you're nuts."

MSF

PLAYBOY: You don't fit most people's image of a devoted biker.

FORBES: I wasn't until I was forty-eight. It happened just by coincidence. One of the guys who worked for me, a chauffeur, a neat guy, wanted to buy a motorcycle and asked if he could borrow the money from me. Well, I told him what most people would have told him, that motorcycling is dangerous and foolish and that he shouldn't do it. Being a sensible man, I tried to talk him out of it. But he bought one anyway and he gave me a ride one day, and the next thing I knew, I was buying many motorcycles for myself and my sons.

PLAYBOY: What is it you love about motorcycles?

FORBES: Traveling on a bike is invariably a delight. I love the exposure to the elements, being part of them instead of boxed off from them, the way you are in a car. It heightens every one of your senses. Your vision is better. Your concentration is better. You're taking more in every moment. It's terrifically invigo-

Here is an ass.

Can an ass fly?

Oh no, an ass cannot fly,

but a good many have tried

in a balloon.

Anonymous, 19th Century

15

rating. Your mind is working on a different beam—all your awarenesses are heightened in a way they aren't in an office, at the desk, on the job. You're like somebody skiing down a slope: totally turned on. I've done some of my best thinking on a motorcycle. It's difficult to jot down your thoughts on a notepad at 70 miles an hour, so the terrific new ideas you get are usually gone with the wind by the time you stop, but some of them stay.

PLAYBOY: What do bikes cost?

FORBES: Oh, I've got bikes that run upwards of $12,000.

PLAYBOY: To most people, that would seem like a lot of money for a motorcycle.

FORBES: It is. But it's not just rich old goats like myself who have those wonderful machines. People who are into bikes are like people who are into rock music. They may not have much else, but they'll have the top-of-the-line speakers, even if it means laying out a month's wages: They'll pay anything they can get their hands on for tickets to the best concerts. So the top-of-the-line bikes are bought, just as often as not, by people whose incomes are small, but this is their dream and their determination, and if you're determined to get something, you do. You just pay the price.

PLAYBOY: How fast do you travel?

FORBES: On the Harley, when you get over about 70, the magic fingers start beating you to pieces. It just vibrates like hell. At the end of the day, you're not about ready to put a quarter in the hotel bed to get some shakes. You've been shaking all day. So as a practical matter, I had the Harley ceiling on me this last trip— just hanging on over 70, the vibes were such that I didn't stay there long. But on the Gold Wing, which was the other bike we had, you can occasionally go in bursts of 110, 115 miles an hour. There's no speed law in Germany and not much of one anywhere else in Europe, so it's legal, it's tempting, and you do it from time to time.

PLAYBOY: We heard you hit 130 once.

FORBES: That was on the Van Veen, the new twin rotary bike from Germany. I got it last summer and my son and I took it out on its first run with Cook Nielson, the editor of *Cycle* mag-

azine, and I wanted to see what its limits were. Well, I got to the bottom of me before I got to the top of the bike, because when I finally worked up the courage to look down at the speedometer and saw what it said, I started getting nervous. And when that happens, you begin to think of little things like blowouts, and you begin to think that this is damned foolishness. Which, of course, it is. At that speed, being careful doesn't do any good. If you have a blowout, you've had it. I didn't stay at 130 very long and I'll promise you and my insurance people right here and now that I'll never do it again.

PLAYBOY: Your motorcycling and ballooning have given you something of a reputation of a daredevil who likes to flirt with danger. Why do you do it?

FORBES: For the sense of the challenge and for the enjoyment. I'm not seeking danger. Sure, it exists, but you minimize it as much as possible, and that's not hard to do. Some people say I must have a death wish, doing these crazy things, but I don't. I'll be the saddest man at my funeral. The last thing I want to do is die; the next time around I can't possibly have it as good as I do this time, so what the hell would I want to check out for? I've got the best this world has to offer. I have no interest in leaving it. I'd never make a good racing-car driver because high speed per se isn't even a source of great satisfaction to me. I don't get that big a kick out of it, except that it is fun to say, "Gee, I did once go . . . that fast." But not for any length of time. It's just an occasional temptation. You look down that open road. There's virtually no traffic. You're trying to cover a long distance. You're exhilarated. And you just find that speedometer creeping up and up. Speed grows on you.

PLAYBOY: That's ironic, because your other main hobby is one of the slowest forms of transportation known to man—balloons.

FORBES: The ballooning happened by coincidence, too. I just happened to read in the local newspaper that there was a fellow offering balloon rides for a price. I had never seen a balloon or been in one, but it sounded like fun and it was right on the way to work, so one morning when we were driving into New York to work, I asked my driver if he'd like to stop for an hour and go for a balloon ride. He said that sounded like a good idea, so we floated around the countryside for an hour and I was in the office by eight-thirty.

PLAYBOY: How did you react to your first balloon ride?

FORBES: It was such a novel experience, a kind of Peter Pan thing. It's so different from flying; it's not flying. You're right in the wind and the air and the clouds—all those forces in nature that come together and have an impact on you and the balloon. You're floating and you're never sure where you're going. In a plane, you gun the engine and flip your flippers and you go up or down and right or left, and it's an immediate response. In a balloon, your sole source of power is a blast of heat, and there's a fifteen-second interval between the blast and when the heat reaches the top of the balloon and you float up. If you stop to think about it, it's like driving a car that doesn't accelerate until fifteen seconds after you hit the gas. Try that sometime. Getting the feeling of the timing in a balloon is one of the extraordinary challenges, and one that captivated me that first day.

You have absolutely no control over your direction. As the wind goes, so go you. It's a unique feeling, combined with the fact that you're seeing a view of the landscape floating slowly beneath you that is different from any view you've ever seen. The whole thing is such a huge turn-on that I have not, with rare exceptions, found anybody who's done it who doesn't love it. You can float just above the treetops, everybody waves at you and yells up, wanting to know where you're going. Well, you don't know where you're going, and even that's an unusual sensation in itself.

On a motorcycle, you sense that not everybody is happy to see you and your mode of transportation going by, but a balloon turns everybody on, with no exceptions. It's a happy thing. People on the ground enjoy seeing this beautiful, unusual thing floating by. What is it? The fact is, it makes no sense. It isn't something to go anyplace in. You get in it and go no place in particular. With a balloon, getting there isn't half the fun; it's all the fun. The trip is the whole trip. The vehicle itself is the thing, the end in itself, not the means of getting somewhere. And all those sensations happen to you the first time you're in one.

I passed the question on the exam but not in the field. I was launching from behind some trees, so we had this lift, saying goodbye to everybody as we rose up so gracefully; then we got up into the cold wind, and we weren't hot enough and the balloon began coming down.

PLAYBOY: Less than a year and a half after your first balloon ride, you set six world records in your cross-country flight. Obviously, you plunged into it.

FORBES: Sure. Once I got into it, I wanted to do the things that hadn't been done. It wasn't just competitive zest. I thought that if you're going to do it at all, you might as well mobilize your resources and have more fun doing what nobody else has done. To keep flying day in and day out you have to have a lot of ground support. You don't know where you're going to land. You fly until you're out of fuel, then you have to have trucks that can get to you. I was dropping tanks to reduce weight—they weigh 20 pounds even empty—and somebody had to retrieve those with a helicopter. Amazing lot of logistics. People can do it on a less expensive scale, but it's harder and takes longer. And what we were doing was taking off from where we landed. That hadn't been done before. You can say you're going to go from West to East, but you can't say you're going from Milwaukee to St. Louis. You can't pick your towns.

PLAYBOY: How did your family react to what you were doing?

FORBES: Enthusiastically. It was an exciting adventure and everybody was in on putting the logistics together. Two of my boys filmed it. A guy named Tracy Barnes had gone cross-country over the period of a year, but it really hadn't been done as a consecutive trip. It was pioneering. I decided it would be fun to try doing it and had the balloon built. The thing got a lot of press coverage because it excited people, and it was the kind of thing where day by day you could follow the progress, or the lack

of it, and it did a whole lot to make people aware of the sport.

Wherever we were, large crowds would come out of the bushes and watch us land, or watch us launch. The most dramatic moment just happened to be when Jack Perkins from NBC News was there and they put it on TV. He was interviewing me at the midway point in some little town in Nebraska. My God, the kids came in their school buses; the whole town came out to watch us launch. We were behind some trees in a field and heating to take off. I'd forgotten a very simple thing: When the wind is rushing over a barrier—such as trees—it creates a false lift, so the balloon would lift before it's hot enough to go, and you're supposed to know that. I passed the question on the exam but not in the field. I was launching from behind some trees, so we had this lift, saying goodbye to everybody as we rose up so gracefully; then we got up in the cold wind and we weren't hot enough and it began coming down. And all this was recorded by NBC. We smashed into one car, bounced, smashed into another car and destroyed five automobiles before we finally lifted off. So Perkins ended up the commentary by saying, "And here are five people who are going to have to tell their insurance companies their cars were smashed by a hit-and-run balloon." God, it was funny and it happened to be captured on film. All this sort of stuff brought a lot of publicity to ballooning. It created a lot of awareness and increased interest in the sport and the drama of it. I got the Harmon Trophy and all these awards that were not in any sense deserved on the merits or the significance; it's just that balloons are such a turn-on.

And all this was recorded by NBC. We smashed into one car, bounced, smashed into another car, and destroyed five automobiles before we finally lifted off. So Perkins ended the commentary by saying, "And

here are five people who are going to have to tell their insurance companies their cars were smashed by a hit-and-run balloon."

1

CHAPTER

A Frenchman Meets the Capitalist Tools

Jean-Lou Colin

FOR TEN DAYS I led the life of a multimillionaire. Of course, personally, I'll never have millions of dollars, but that's not the point. I spent ten days sharing practically every minute in the life of one of the richest men in the United States (and therefore the world).

Perhaps, like me before I met him, the name Malcolm S. Forbes isn't familiar to you; however, there's hardly anyone in America who doesn't know who he is, mainly because of his wealth. His yacht, Maserati, Lamborghini and his Boeing 727 are only the tip of the iceberg, a fact that does not become apparent until you realize the extent of his estates: the palace in Morocco, the house in London, the chateau in Normandy, and various ranches in the United States, all offering a good choice of weekend retreats. Oh, and I forgot to mention the island in Fiji. It is only eighteen miles wide and I doubt that the local taxes are very high there. On the other hand, I don't know how they tax works of art in the United States, but I'm sure, considering what a keen collector Malcolm is, that the American government is not doing too badly on him on that score! Apart from a huge collection of paintings, some much more valuable than others, he owns a very impressive collection of objects made by Peter Carl Fabergé for the Imperial Russian family (the famous Fabergé eggs). This collection is as large as that owned by the Kremlin and must certainly be worth millions. Not to mention his collections of toy soldiers and toy boats, deemed to be the most beautiful in the world.

Having said all that, if Malcolm Forbes is one of the most respected men in his own country, it is not so much for his immense wealth but for the magazine which he edits and which is named after him (or rather, after his father, B. C. Forbes, who founded it in 1917): *Forbes* magazine.

With a circulation of 725,000, this bimonthly magazine is the American businessman's bible. In a land where money is the most important thing, Malcolm Forbes, the great advocate of free enterprise and capitalism (he calls his magazine "The Capitalist Tool"), is regarded somewhat as the kingpin of business and economics.

Gold threads on red denim are "colors" not apt to be confused with those of Hell's Angels.

It is not, however, just because he is rich and famous, that we at *Moto-Journal* are interested in Malcolm Forbes. Of course he has plenty of money, but he also has some great toys.

In fact, he has two hobbies: ballooning (hot-air ballooning, to be precise) and motorcycling, both of which he carries out on an equally grand scale. Take the motorbikes—he has about seventy in his garage, or rather, his garages. Not just for decoration, either. Absolutely not. These are working motorbikes (most of them equipped with radar detectors), and someone is employed more or less just to look after this incredible array of bikes. Lots of Harleys, of course, but also quite a few sporty models, such as Bimota, CB 1100 R, Van Veen, Vetter Mystery Ship, BMW Krauser, Munch, etc.

Malcolm rides a motorbike regularly, even in New York, and despite the fact that he came to the sport quite late in life, at age forty-eight, he has some impressive trips to his credit. For a start, he was the first Westerner to cross

the U.S.S.R. and China on a motorbike, with the bikes flying the American flag and everyone wearing T-shirts with the slogan "Capitalist Tool" emblazoned on them. You can call that provocation, evangelism or just simply strong patriotism—either way, the whole thing is very well done.

Seemingly unconcerned about the size of his balloons, Malcolm has had one made for him that measures 115 feet. It is an exact replica of his chateau in Balleroy, Normandy, where he has a ballooning museum and where, every year, he holds an international balloon meeting. I've seen this huge balloon flying, and I can tell you it really is an amazing sight.

In the same way as with his bikes, Malcolm isn't content to just potter around at home with his balloons. In 1973 he made the first coast-to-coast crossing of the United States in a balloon, a journey of 3,100 miles that took thirty-four

Patches—back and front—sometimes have fellow bikers asking, "What kind of tools do you make?"

days, that earned him the continuing respect of his peers. When he went to Pakistan by motorbike, he had a 100-meter-high balloon made in the shape of a minaret; and when he went to China he brought with him, along with five (yes, I did say five) of his motorbikes, a balloon. The balloon was transported in a van behind the cavalcade of bikes.

My story all started at the office on a beautiful June day. Thanks to our dear boss, Pierre Barret, who had met with him in Paris, we received a charming letter from a certain Mr. Forbes, inviting a member of the staff to join him and his friends for a little bit of motorcycling in the United States. Because of my command of the language of Shakespeare (!) and the fact that I was free to travel, in the end I was the lucky one to go. Off I went to America, without really thinking about what I was doing or whom I was going to meet and what I would be doing once I got there. I just thought, well, ten days' holiday in the States; that sounds pretty good, and I can always pop over afterwards to see my friends in California.

I had been given an address on Fifth Avenue in New York, and when we pulled up there, I had the first intimation of what was in store for me: I could barely see the top of the building in front of me. It was almost a skyscraper, and it was the Forbes Building.

A nice pied-à-terre! It was only the first of an accumulation of astonishing things which piled up, one on top of the other, during my trip. All together, they would give me some small idea of the scope of the man I was about to meet that first day, Malcolm Forbes. He inspires respect, but at the same time one can see in his look that relaxed simplicity which makes Americans so easy to get along with. Less than an hour after meeting him, we were in a supermarket together like old friends. He was pushing the cart and asking me what I wanted for dinner. I could have thought that I was simply a reporter who was going to share a few minutes in the life of a very busy man, but I soon happily realized that

It took Mansard 20 years (1600–1620) to build what British balloon maker Don Cameron did in 20 weeks.

I was going to be treated as an honored guest. I must say that this prodigal hospitality for a total stranger is a bit troubling, even perhaps embarrassing, for us Frenchmen with our ingrained reserve. Americans do have some qualities that are less than endearing, but this is not one of them.

With the groceries piled up in the padded trunk of a splendid Maserati Quattroprote, we took off for Timberfield, the Forbes estate in New Jersey. The house is large and very comfortable but not particularly luxurious: No marble bathrooms with gold-plated faucets: Timberfield is a house to live in. In any case, there isn't any reason for Malcolm to show off. Everyone, at least over there, knows that he is rich.

At table, the same simplicity. There is a bottle of Chateau Margaux '53 in my honor but no butler to pour it, and if the gardener and the mechanic happen to be around at dinnertime, they are invited to share the meal.

Just looking at the menu, you realize that this is not exactly a communistic life, but with Forbes there is a paradoxical feeling of having reached a supreme state of socialism: There is so much money that it seems to have no value and almost not to exist. In addition, millionaires are probably a godsend to the unemployed. Between his various properties, hobbies, and multifarious activities, not to mention the magazine, Malcolm must employ at the very least six hundred people. Just imagine that there is a team of men who do nothing but take care of the balloons, taking them around from one show to another, and so on! Last year, twenty-eight of them came to France for the yearly meet at Balleroy. True enough, Malcolm likes to share his pleasures—that's why he invited me.

If a careful inspection of the garage, where about thirty machines were impeccably lined up, hadn't convinced me, visits to the local dealers would have. Malcolm is a gold star customer. Not only does he buy almost everything with a capacity of over 750 cc, but one bike or another is always being modified or repaired in every shop.

By himself, he wouldn't be able to put much

mileage on all of them, even if he drove more than he does. The following day I would learn about that.

That Sunday, he had organized a "poker run," a kind of rally in which everyone in the neighborhood who can drive is invited to participate. They are men neither of his own age nor on his level. Instead, it's the gardener and his pals, and their pals. Except for Malcolm's own, there can't be many millionaires' sons in the group.

After filling up at the private pump, everyone puts on vests with the clan colors, and embroidered "Capitalist Tools" (and not, as you can well imagine, "Hell's Angels"!).

Malcolm, wearing black leather and a black helmet, is the "leader of the pack," at the head of a well-disciplined group. Even on the open highway, they stick to the 55 mph speed limit (except for a few who rev up to a daring 70 mph in a moment of madness!). The whole day will go by this way. True, the weather is marvelous, and the countryside is beautiful, but on the Harley XR 1000 that was assigned to me the pace is a bit boring. What a pack of thirty bikes like this would be like on the road in France, I'm almost afraid to imagine. The amusing thing about it is that I truly believe that the men who are doing 65 or 70 mph today really think they are going fast.

We check in at a supermarket parking area. Then the run begins. You cruise along a predetermined itinerary, stopping at five control points, at each of which you draw a card from a poker deck.

On Sunday mornings, out of this capitalist's stable no polo ponies but packs of horsepower.

We end in a clearing, where there is a barbecue and where prizes are distributed to the
highest poker draws. Two pairs to the ace win
a can of oil offered by the Machpro Station;
three kings get you a sissy bar from the Harley
dealer. It's all very nice, even if some of the
riders have looks that might make you want to
cross to the other side of the street in other
circumstances. Here, motorcycling is above all
a social game: don't scrape the road on the
curves trying to pull ahead—just be one of the
group. Surprising, nevertheless, to see a gentleman like Malcolm Forbes drinking beer with a
gang of "outlaws."

On Monday, with me still on the Harley of
course, we take off for Pennsylvania to drop in
at the Harley-Davidson factory in York, for the
presentation of the 1984 line to the dealers. As
a professional journalist I wasn't allowed to go
along with Malcolm while he tried out the famous prototype with a Porsche V4 motor. As a
consolation, I was allowed to try out the new
models on the private track at the factory, along
with the dealers. The track is narrow and full of
curves and you are asked not to go over 50 mph,
and no passing a driver in front of you! So much
for American test drives. They have a great
time, though! There is a difference between
Kenny Roberts and the average American motorcyclist, even a 45-degree-angle difference.
Americans are not given to violence, and they
are so obsessed with the idea of safety that they
don't allow any room for reflex action or initia-
tive. Whether in cars or on motorcycles, the
Americans are without doubt the worst drivers
on the planet. I think, by the way, that the only
thing that interests the men who are there is
whether the vibration on the new V2 is as good
as on the old one. Malcolm isn't really sold on
the V4 and decides to stick with the evolution-
ary 2 cylinder, at least for the time being. So
now he places his order: "Vaughn, give me a
Softail, an FXRS, and an . . . FXSB. I'd like to
take them with me, if possible."

"Of course, Malcolm. And we'll take the old
ones you came on back to Timberfield for you."
A couple of small purchases for $20,000—even
in the States Harleys aren't cheap—at least,
not always: that night, during the big reception

given for the dealers, Harley Davidson gives
Malcolm the one model he didn't order from the
'84 line: an FXRT, in recognition of the marvelous publicity he has given the company during
his worldwide trips.

And so we go back to Timberfield on motorcycles just off the production line and not yet
available to the public.

The next day we flew first class by United
Airlines to Denver in Colorado and Jackson
Hole in Wyoming, where one of the Forbes
ranches is, at the gates of the famous Yellow-
stone National Park. An ideal location for a
film. Only a few hundred meters away, the
Snake River rushes noisily on, and at any minute I half expected to see a band of wild Indians
paddling by. In the meantime I stretched out
on the porch of my own private log cabin, enjoying an unparalleled view of the Grand Teton.
We'll have more opportunity to savor these terrific Rocky Mountain landscapes on the way to
Riverton, a town about 180 miles away, to at-

A Frenchman Meets the Capitalist Tools · 27

Gas is where it's at for bikes, balloons, or baked beans. Bertie Forbes (far left): cooking with her gas while MSF gets high on his.

tend a big balloon meet. The road is superb, and our bikes, a Venture, an Aspencade, and a 1300 Kawasaki (Malcolm is vexed by the non-delivery of a Voyager he had ordered), which tend to look positively elephantine in tamer surroundings, are perfectly at home in this grandiose setting. They really seem to belong, and are a pleasure to drive. Their size seems completely natural to the bikers in the area: they even hook on trailers to carry their camping equipment. We got back from Riverton just in time to sit down to a "local color" meal cooked by Mrs. Forbes. Although married to a millionaire and born a millionaire (she is a Laidlaw, and they were among the great Wall Street banking families), she won't let anyone else do the cooking or even the washing up. If it's airs and graces you want, you'll have to look elsewhere. Right now, there is a meal to enjoy, and to surprise a French palate: ham served with bright green peas and sweet potatoes with marshmallow topping! Worth the trip! And then, to wind up a perfect day, we go to have a farewell drink at the Cowboy Million Dollar Bar in Jackson Hole.

The next day, the Forbes clan heads back East, where work is waiting.

Horsepower is relative: le cowboy *Jean-Luc and his two mounts.*

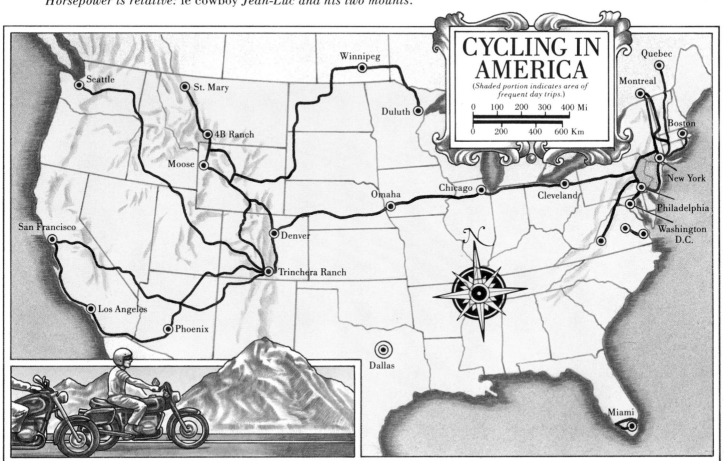

CYCLING IN
AMERICA

(*Shaded portion indicates area of
frequent day trips.*)

0   100   200   300   400 Mi

0   200   400   600 Km

2

CHAPTER

AMERICA
From
Coast to Coast

Gordon Cruikshanks

ANYONE SAILING the cold, shallow waters off little Gwynn Island in the mouth of the Chesapeake Bay at precisely ten minutes after two in the afternoon of November 6, 1973, would have witnessed an astounding sight—and forget your flying saucers and little green men. For descending upon him would have been a huge blue-and-gold gored hot-air balloon mysteriously about to splash down in the middle of nowhere. He might even have noted, in his confusion, the huge sign on the great bag: "Forbes Magazine"—or perhaps its name, *Chateau de Balleroy*, Forbes's chateau situated 20 miles from Normandy Beach in France. Maybe even the numbers N1626, the date when the chateau had been built.

Peering down at him over the rim of the basket would have been two strangely clad figures: Malcolm Forbes, whose thing—or at least one of many—is ballooning of the most adventuresome sort, and his son Robert. Actually, the balloon had come all the way from Coos Bay in Oregon, where it had floated aloft 34 bruising days before, and was now fulfilling Forbes's dream of a Coast-to-Coast record (the FIRST!) in his own balloon. He had set six other world records on the way. To go from sea to sea it had taken twenty-one flights totaling 2,911 statute miles with an in-air time of only 141 hours and 30 minutes. Riding his giant hot-air bubble, as high as 17,400 feet at one point over the western mountains, and careening along in the jet stream at 66 mph at another, Forbes had pitted teamwork, tenacity, planning, and mindboggling logistics—for any balloonist—against his personal mountain and had won. Now he held one of aeronautical history's greatest Firsts—a Coast-to-Coast crossing in the same balloon.

Only one man before had tried the Herculean task: Tracy Barnes had made his own valiant Jules Verne voyage back in 1966, but it had taken him five months, two balloons and a month's stay in a San Diego hospital before he completed his transcontinental flight in stages. Barnes's effort was somewhat reminiscent of

A sign now marks the trip's launch site on the coast of Oregon.

"I Thought You Were the First to Balloon Across America?"

After Maxie Anderson's spectacular achievement in ballooning from San Francisco to Canada's Gaspé Peninsula, which was media-hailed as a "first," many have said they recollected that my cross-country balloon venture of seven years ago was the first.

It was—and Maxie's was.

You see, there are two *totally different* types of ballooning: hot air, which (appropriately, I'm sure FORBES readers would agree) was what I used to successfully cross the U.S., and gas (helium), which is what enabled Maxie to cross both the Atlantic and North America nonstop.

Hot-air ballooning is overwhelmingly prevalent because, for a $9 tankful of propane, you can enjoy a 45-minute flight. Because these tanks are heavy, hot-air balloons are limited in how many persons they can carry, how long they can stay up. On our cross-country trip, I set the then world record for a hot-air balloon aloft—13 hours and 5 minutes. It took us 21 arduous days of flying *(see map)* to accomplish this first and still only such voyage.

To fill a helium balloon costs $1,000 to $2,000 and, to come down, the thousands of dollars' worth must be vented away. But, when filled and with sufficient ballast, a gas balloon can stay aloft for many days—the world record is held by Maxie and his two Atlantic-crossing colleagues, 5 days, 17 hours.

The father-and-son Anderson crossing of North America is indeed a fabulous first. Our town trip was, too, a first in fact, different in kind—and, as with most everything past, is fading in memory.

—Malcolm Forbes

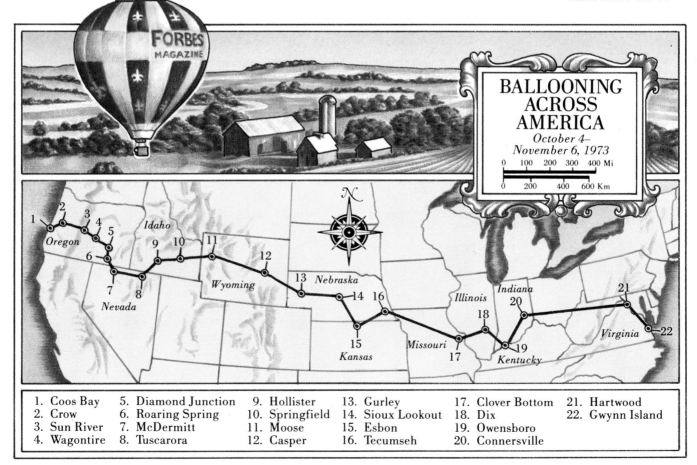

BALLOONING ACROSS AMERICA
October 4–November 6, 1973

0   100   200   300   400 Mi

0   200   400   600 Km

1. Coos Bay	5. Diamond Junction	9. Hollister	13. Gurley	17. Clover Bottom	21. Hartwood
2. Crow	6. Roaring Spring	10. Springfield	14. Sioux Lookout	18. Dix	22. Gwynn Island
3. Sun River	7. McDermitt	11. Moose	15. Esbon	19. Owensboro	
4. Wagontire	8. Tuscarora	12. Casper	16. Tecumseh	20. Connersville	

Calbraith Rogers battering his way east to west in a crash-by-crash airplane crossing in the early part of the century. Barnes made it, but after the well-organized Forbes feat, his mark now is a historical asterisk.

Everything connected with Forbes—the man himself, his incredible multifaceted enterprises, and his ballooning—is larger than life. His widely publicized First came only fifteen months after his first ride in a balloon, back in July of 1972. With but 33.5 hours in his logbook prior to his coast-to-coast attempt he had already created a "Balloon Ascension Division."

In spite of his swift ascent in the world of ballooning, he lacked neither ability nor capability for a record performance. With Forbes, thought translates into action, action into quick and uncommon events. He flew his "check in" flight to the world of hot-air ballooning in July 1972, at Princeton, New Jersey, with Phil Hallstein, then rapidly built up air time, mostly by weekend ballooning from his home in Far Hills, New Jersey. Total family involvement is the key. He was now flying two balloons: *The Roberta*, a 50-footer named after Mrs. Forbes, and *The Moira*, a 60-footer named for his daughter. In rapid succession Forbes and his family tied for second place in the first Great Kentucky Derby Festival Balloon Race in Louisville last April; came in second in the Great Export "A" Balloon Race in Toronto, Canada, in June. And in the same month he entered two balloons in a field of nine in the First Bahamas-to-Florida Balloon Race. Forbes placed third for the over-the-Gulfstream journey in less than six hours. Thus, prior to his Coast-to-Coast attempt, Malcolm Forbes had built up considerable balloon time.

Then one day he made a historical phone call. As balloon buffs know, Paul E. (Ed) Yost, president of Dakota Industries, Inc., Sioux Falls, South Dakota, is a wizard of the balloon-building art. His company had built the famous Lark Cigarette balloon. But let one of Yost's associates tell the story.

"We were at the April Kentucky Derby Balloon Race, and we got a telephone call from someone named Forbes who said he was interested in having Ed build a special, super hot-air balloon. Well, Ed gets lots of calls like that, and we go along with the gag because when it gets into the numbers (money) we never hear of them again. But this turned out, as you know, different!"

Ed Yost, who is justly called the father of modern-day ballooning and probably has more balloon patents than anyone else in the world, had some interesting proposals for Forbes. What Yost proposed was a size-rated Sub-Class AX-8, the definition established by the National Aeronautic Association—that is, under 100,000 cu. ft. It would be able to stay aloft almost twice as long as any other balloon of its class—as well as the next two categories! Forbes made an on-the-spot decision. And that is how the now historic balloon called the *Chateau de Balleroy* (pronounced Ba-luh-wah) was conceived, built, and flown in a few short months into the world record books.

It didn't take Ed Yost long to "get with" the program. The Forbes Ascension Division soon had the world's first $25,000 (reportedly) hot-air balloon. It took only six weeks to design and fabricate the stunning blue-and-gold balloon. Fifty-eight feet in diameter and 65 feet high, it held 95,000 cu. ft. of hot air. The job wasn't easy. After the 1.4-ounce coated fabric was received it had been dyed blue and gold, gores plotted and cut. Sewing ran far into the night— many of them. Complicating the task—the real "secret" of *Chateau de Balleroy*—was an inner layer of aluminized fabric, which provided a six-inch air space between itself and the outer envelope. Its purpose was to reflect heat inward. This unique heat-retention feature Yost calculated could keep the balloon aloft almost twenty hours. That he was correct is proved in the record book.

When Forbes was asked how he did not freeze on the 17,400 foot hop over the mountains—while sucking oxygen—he said, "Are you kidding? The warm air coming down out of the bag was great, no problem whatsoever."

Some interesting things came to light as the Odyssey gradually unfolded across the nation. For instance, it was originally thought that the flight could be accomplished at the average altitude of two to three thousand feet. But only

While this hot-air balloon stands 65 feet tall, the dry October mountains of Idaho put it in a different perspective.

four of the twenty-one days were flown under 3,000 feet. The average came out 8,000 to 10,000—the highest 17,400. This cut the planned twenty-hour cruise potential in half.

Another surprise for most was the steadily increasing ground speeds as the trip moved eastward, even though more than once as the balloon descended to land, the lower winds would be blowing east to west. This happened on the first officially observed leg, that was flown to a new distance record of 213 statute miles between Casper, Wyoming, and Gurley, Nebraska. On reaching about 1,500 feet above ground, the "Ba-luh-wah" made almost a complete circle before touching down on Arnold Draper's farm.

The roughest segment was flown over Esbon, Kansas, where clear turbulence set Forbes and some tanks rattling around the gondola like dice in a cup. Crosswind gusts were so rough that Forbes had a flame-out at 8,000 feet. The tense

moment was matched only later when the *Chateau de Balleroy* became partially impaled on power lines near Fredericksburg, Virginia.

"I think the thing that really saved us there was probably that the initial contact shorted out the lines and blew the overload switches at the power stations. But even so, it was a delicate situation," recalls Forbes, who also had a friend's son as a passenger—his first trip in a hot-air balloon.

When NAA's official observer Randy Randleman joined the party at North Platte, Nebraska, he, unlike your reporter, who flew in the "chase plane," traveled with the ground convoy. As the expedition moved eastward it became more difficult for them to stay in constant sight of the balloon. But Randy managed to be on the spot to certify the new record for distance of 312 miles between Tecumseh, Nebraska, and Union, Missouri, and the new duration record of thirteen hours and five minutes between North Platte, Nebraska and Esbon, Kansas. A good day's work!

It was unfortunate that no NAA official could be present to verify the record when Malcolm

The chase crew watch the NBC camera crew shoot the balloon over the Midwest. The steel-framed gondola carried fifteen propane tanks when seeking to set records.

Forbes with passengers hit the fantastic speeds of 56 and 46 mph on the last two legs of the journey. At one time on the 416-mile flight between Connersville, Indiana, and Hartwood, Virginia, speeds up to 66 mph were registered! When questioned about whether it might be worthwhile to return to Connersville next year at the same time to take a chance on catching the same winds, a smiling Forbes conceded it might be a good idea—before some weekend flyer got the idea.

The first ten days after the noon lift-off at Coos Bay, Oregon, on October 4, were really tough going with lots of yo-yoing but not much mileage racked up. In fact, only 788 miles had been flown up to October 15. For the first two flights, Ed Yost, the designer, went along as copilot to make sure the equipment was functioning properly. For the next eight hops the copilot chores were taken over by James Craig, of Ridgecrest, California. Craig is the director

America from Coast to Coast · 37

Your flight across the United States has been a subject of interest to many, I am sure, but I am wondering if you realize as you wend your way across this land, how many lives you are touching. On this morning of Oct. 22, I came out of my house on my way to school (I teach English to high school seniors) and saw your balloon in the far western sky. It was a beautiful sunshiny morning, and there in the sky was a new and unusual phenomenon. About 8:10 my students began arriving in class, and they gathered at the windows and doors to watch you. By this time, you were north and east of the school building. Many had never seen a balloon before and were fascinated with your journey. Teenagers are by nature intrigued by adventure, and here you were floating across their world—slowly and surely—being able to look down upon all humanity and close enough and slowly enough to note their activities.

Their comments were many and varied but all curious: "Gee, what a trip!" "I wonder if he gets cold up there." "Does he have a parachute?" "What do you suppose he eats?" "How does he steer it?" "Does he ever travel at night?" "Are there lights on the balloon?" "How big is the basket?" "Does it have a roof?" "What furniture does he have in there?" "Boy, I wish we could see it up close." So on and on they talked as they watched you float by—a superman, not from outer space but right here in near space. One boy who lives in the country even drove a few miles north of his home so that he was under the balloon as it passed.

Mr. Don Osborn, our principal, had been to North Platte to try to see the balloon on Sunday as he was especially interested in the flight. He joined in the watch here this morning. By 9:30 you were east and south of us and going merrily on your sunny way. We watched you out of sight. As you crossed Cozad, Neb. and our high school, how could you be aware that we were gazing at you with wonder and awe, a little bit of the past in our modern world?

I am writing to tell you, Mr. Forbes, that we were glad that Cozad, Neb. was on your itinerary because for a few moments, you brought the magic of another era into our lives.

—Betty Menke

of the experimental balloon research program for the U.S. Navy and is a qualified NAA observer.

"The first ten days of the trip were hell—with a few pleasant exceptions like Sun River," says Don Garson of *Forbes*, who acted as project public relations and coordinator. "Malcolm Forbes floated from farms to ranches to desert land that everyone warned us only a hermit could love. Everyone warned us about the Cascade Mountains and the Rockies, but it was the Steen Mountains in between that caused the most difficulty.

An evening touchdown in Oregon's flatlands, a time for tents and sleeping bags.

In a millions-to-one chance, the cross-country balloon landed on the Jackson, Wyoming, Rockefeller ranch, just a mile from the Forbes family's Grand Teton summer cabin.

While we received a warm welcome and great news coverage prior to our departure from Coos Bay, you can imagine the press response we received from places like Crow, Sun River, Wagontire, Frenchglen, Diamond Junction and Roaring Spring in Oregon, and McDermitt and Tuscarora in Nevada!"

At Moose, Jackson Hole, Wyoming, Forbes tried to land in front of his own cabin, which he and Mrs. Forbes built more than twenty years ago. But a sudden updraft carried him into some pines on the nearby Rockefeller ranch. When this reporter joined the party two days later at Pocatello, Idaho, the crew was still raving about the dinner that Mrs. Forbes cooked for eighteen, and how Jerry Melsha, associated with Ed Yost, had that same night sewed up the damaged *Chateau de Balleroy*.

After Forbes's takeoff from Jackson with Dick Keuser as copilot on the morning of the sixteenth, that beautiful gold Convair 580 turboprop picked up your reporter and the NAA observer at the Pocatello Airport. Flying the *Capitalist Tool* were two ex-Air Force pilots, Joe Eberhardt, captain, and Jim Butler. With them were Marvin Shimp on leave from the U.S. Weather Service; and, of course, the two Forbes boys, Bob and Tim, who were loaded down with movie and still cameras to record every phase of the historic project. They ended up shooting more than 40,000 feet of movie film.

It seemed a matter of minutes until we were circling the *Chateau de Balleroy*—already at 14,500 feet and in minus 20-degree centigrade cold on a beautifully clear day. Malcolm and Dick had just passed Gannett Peak, and, with

America from Coast to Coast · 39

the distant snow-capped Grand Teton it was truly an inspiring sight. But it looked as if they literally were steering the balloon along Route 26 and 26/20 up to the doorstep at Casper Airport. With a few gallons more fuel they could have landed on the airport only a few miles away.

This 7-hour 26-minute leg covered 163 miles and left less than five gallons usable fuel before touching down. The longest leg flown so far, it was the fastest at 21.8 mph. During all legs of the flight the Convair circled to stay within sight of the balloon—often slowing and dropping some flaps while shooting their pictures. Most of the time the *Capitalist Tool* would land about two hours ahead on the flight track. Then things happened. Don Garson could get to a phone to call the press—his airborne suitcase phone didn't perform very well within the aircraft. He'd call ahead and reconfirm hotel, motel accommodations for eighteen to twenty-one people (the task force varied from time to time).

The stop would save fuel. The balloon would take at least one-and-a-half hours approaching, and about the same time going past, clearly in view all the time. Cars and people seemed to spring out of the plains from nowhere when the *Chateau de Balleroy* hove in sight. And by touchdown time in the early evening, the roads began to clog up along the path at the random touchdown point.

The price wasn't all financial—about $100,000. It was physical, too. For thirty-four days Malcolm S. Forbes took the beating of his life. Meeting him for the first time at the Showboat Motel right after the Casper, Wyoming, landing, we found him black and blue from high on the chest down to his calves! Recent bruises

Built by Ed Yost, the father of modern hot-air ballooning, the Chateau de Balleroy *with Forbes as pilot broke six world records.*

were bluish black. The older ones were beginning to fade to a grayish cast. In spite of long john underwear, padded leather jumpsuit, sweaters, and a heavy fur parka, rattling around with a dozen propane tanks inside of a two-man gondola that hits the ground at at least 25 mph, then being pulled or dumped on its side, and dragged until the envelope collapses, is a rough experience—repeated over and over.

On this evening, everyone was extremely pleased and elated with the first really long flight and the feeling that they were really "out of the woods." We could now "run downhill to the Atlantic—anywhere between Maine and Florida will be fine by me, but we would like to hit the Jersey shore," said Forbes.

The next day he was to establish his first officially observed world record—later broken—but first about the plan. It was simple. Jerry Melsha would stay up late and sew together two nine-foot canopy parachutes so that the two extra gallon tanks could be used for takeoff and climb to cruise altitude and then dropped, to be picked up by the Bell 47 helicopter. Also, the first leg was to be flown solo in order to increase distance and flight duration. It worked beautifully! The 213-mile record could not have been made that day without those extra tanks, because it took almost an hour to get away from the Casper area before picking up the right winds. After that agonizing slow start, Forbes made his fastest time until then, averaging 22.3 mph.

Except for the bout with the power lines in Virginia, the rest of the trip must have seemed psychologically easy—after all, there were the words "Downhill all the way to the Atlantic." Perhaps it seemed that way after scaling the real mountains. It may have been long as the crow but not time flies until descending into the Chesapeake, at the edge of the Atlantic on that November 6 afternoon—but there the *Cha-*
(continued on page 44)

A Dozen Years Ago, I Thought Son Bob and I Were Freezing

in the waters of the Chesapeake Bay at the end of the first transcontinental hot-air balloon flight. On that last day high winds were blowing us straight out the Chesapeake's wide mouth into the Atlantic. There seemed more likelihood of fishing boats and prompt rescue in the Bay, so down we splashed. In 21 days of flying since taking off at the edge of the Pacific on Coos Bay, Oregon, we'd set six world records.

Though all those records have been exceeded, no one's made another such transcontinental voyage since. Nor would I again. As I said as much as ten years ago, "The Why Nots are multitudinous and range from the requirement for unlimited luck, ridiculous expense, considerable planning and five weeks of time in the doing to the limitless uselessness of the accomplishment."

In recollection, it seems like the proverbial yesterday. But 'twixt then and now, three more daughters-in-law, a son-in-law and five granddaughters have joined our clan. Since such happy events do take time, I guess that the takeoff in Coos Bay really couldn't have been yesterday.

Final touchdown in the Chesapeake.

Longest Day's Journey

AHEAD STRETCHED hundreds of miles of relatively flat land at low elevations, with nothing to impede speed if the winds would blow strong. So in the dark just before 6:00 A.M. of Thursday morning, October 25, I lifted off in some really swinging winds of great promise, with fifteen fuel tanks instead of the regular twelve.

Normally, flying in the dark doesn't make it too difficult to see where one's going. The spread-out towns are lit and, from on high, it's easy to decide which is which so long as your takeoff site is fixed in your mind.

That was the rub that morning.

The speeding winds, so essential to the day's objective, were whirling me around like a slow top. While seven revolutions a minute may be slow for a top, it was crazy fast for a balloon.

For a few minutes I was able to keep track, headed northwest at a happy speed with the lights from half a dozen towns visible. Soon, however, I was feeling a little dizzy and completely disoriented. Lost, but not too worried, I knew within an hour or so it would be light and easier to figure out if the balloon was over Nebraska or Iowa or Missouri or Kansas. Any one of these four states was a possibility.

Until then, confidence in my navigating ability had grown at a steady, heady rate. But when you've been up in a balloon for only an hour over the great middle of our country and can't figure out which of four states you are in, it modifies one's navigational conceit.

As day dawned, I was still in the dark.

Finally a ribbon of water showed up. As we got closer, it got wider, and even I was certain it was the wide Missouri River. Since the *Balleroy* was west of it, there were only two possibilities; either Nebraska or Kansas. Pretty deductive, eh? At the Missouri's edge I was over a sizable city and further narrowed the location—it had to be either Leavenworth or Atchison. Any fool could figure out which, but since I was no fool, I couldn't.

Do you know what finally clued me in?

Forbes searches for a way to avoid the water below.

On the west bank the chart had a clear symbol indicating a stadium. Low and behold, when over it, I recognized it, and that meant Atchison! Radio contact had been intermittently maintained with the ground vehicles and, to their occasional query about the balloon's whereabouts, I pretended not to hear or mumbled so the words couldn't be understood. By the time I could answer "Atchison," they were far behind and out of range. The helicopter was God knows where. It couldn't take off until daylight and then the pilot hadn't any more idea as to where he should head than I had had about where the balloon was.

Once again, getting rid of empty tanks presented a problem that needed solving as promptly as possible. With the prospect of breaking the *Balleroy*'s own week-old distance record getting better with every fast-flying minute, I hoped to make the new one a really good one and needed to get rid of the extra weight. With a third of the country still to cross, I didn't want to jettison these tanks without someone to retrieve 'em. If lost, who knew how long it would take to replace them with their special fittings.

With no possibility of help from the helicopter or ground crew, the *Tool* tried by radio to charter a chopper from huge Kansas International Airport, but none was available. The chance to really smash the distance record was dimmer if I couldn't dump the unneeded weight.

Then occurred one of those happy events that sometimes do happen at a time of problems.

From a major Air Force base, visible some thirty miles south, came the call "Fox Mike 60 [radio lingo for *Tool*], the Kansas National Guard has a helicopter that can reach you in twenty minutes, and they've volunteered to help if you'd like it."

"*Like it?!*" I replied with audible joy, and in less than twenty minutes that beautiful whirlybird was below and ready for the drops, which came in rapid succession—one, two, three, four and five. The *Tool* rendezvoused with them for the pickup, unbounded appreciation was expressed to the Kansas National Guard in general and their two crackerjack choppermen in particular. By 1:00 P.M. the "old" 213-mile distance record was surpassed, and reaching St. Louis 150 miles away seemed possible. As the afternoon dwindled, though, so did wind and light, and I landed in Clover Bottom, some sixty miles southwest of St. Louis. The *Balleroy*'s new world record for distance in a hot-air balloon was exactly one hundred miles greater, officially observed, barographically recorded. And, incidentally, for a second time the old Time Aloft record had been broken.

Friday's run was to be a short one, because that afternoon we had to head once more for New York and some business catch-up. It was our energetically cheerful strongman Kip Cleland's turn to fly. We made a pleasant 115-mile beeline past Saint Louis to Dix, Illinois. On this landing there was a new twist—no wind at all. Fifty feet above the ground I had to stop because the balloon was over trees. We just hung there and hung there at treetop level until every treetop was intimately familiar. Finally we inched over a small clearing and, while I vented on one side, Kip vented on the other, and we dropped the short remaining distance to the ground at the speed of a rock.

First on the scene was a great hulk of a man with a flabbily cherubic face. Wrapped around his torso was a holster complete with pistol whose handle stuck into his armpit. "This is a balloon, huh? How about giving a guy a ride in it?" We didn't know if he was the farm owner, the law or a real live *Of Mice and Men* Lenny. We parried his request while he carried on a nonstop rambling monologue. When the actual

farm owner and numerous neighbors arrived, the hulk handed out his card, identifying him as a traveling Electrolux salesman. The constant way he lovingly fingered that loaded revolver made me think that occasionally to an all-alone farm-wife his sales argument must have been persuasive.

—Malcolm Forbes

teau de Balleroy was at long last, out of its element but safely upon the water. Much remains between these lines.

The Forbes record seems destined to last—although all records exist to be broken. The crew—the total crew, aloft in the accompanying plane, as well as on the ground—to say nothing of the magnificent balloon with its double envelope, testified adequately that no balloonist confined to weekend flying, or without the impressive logistics, would stand a chance of duplicating the Forbes Odyssey within the same time span. Forbes might conceivably have pressed on—but the wide Atlantic was ahead.

Why does Malcolm Forbes do it? Why did he imagine this Twentieth Century Odyssey across the continent's width of air ocean? There's more than one clue in this publisher's (Forbes's) statement:

"All other sport just cannot compare! Ballooning has everything!—the constant challenges; the unusual excitement it creates, even to the ground observer; the aesthetics and, of course, it is also a team sport. What more can anyone ask for?" he declared.

That's hard to top. As is the fabulous FIRST.

Last Day's Journey

THE DAY FOLLOWING a third distance record—and, incidentally, a collision with a power line near Fredericksburg, Virginia—was one for repairing, not flying. By 9:00 A.M., All Hands were in the parachute center's hangar spreading out the *Balleroy* and examining its wounds. Close examination turned up only two tiny burn marks, but there were seven tears, one sizable. It was not as bad as I had anticipated from the rough manhandling we'd had to give the envelope while getting it off the power lines and pole.

Out of the Mercedes came sewing machine, patching material and extra fabric and by day's end our experienced Fleck had the job completed. The inner balloon, that top-half lining of thin silver fabric, had been much weakened during the course of the journey on those several occasions when we had unknowingly and sometimes unavoidably overheated. It had frayed spots, tears, and some loose hanging pieces, but there was no way that much could be done about these. And, until inflation again, we couldn't be certain how seriously further torn that inner balloon was.

Part of the equipment needed to fly a balloon across the U.S. is an industrial sewing machine . . . very handy when there's just one more day to go.

Meantime Harry Schoelpple, a nearby parachuting enthusiast who had built his Hartwood Field into a sizable center for the sport, was lining up needed propane and accumulating weather forecasts for Monday—mostly bad. Rain, wrong-way winds, cloud cover—all the things weather shouldn't be for ballooning. Back at the motel Don Garson, who'd spent five weeks either pressing or being pressed by the press, was busy making arrangements for an increasing number who wanted to cover the final leg of the trip. Our old friends from NBC/TV were coming in Sunday evening. The *New York Times* was sending one of its special feature writers and a photographer, and the wire services as well as the area press wanted to know where and when the takeoff was to be. The final leg to the Atlantic shore was not likely to be more than 170 miles if the wind blew northward to Cape May, not more than 135 miles if it blew east toward Ocean City, and not more than 150 miles if it blew southeast below Norfolk.

As so often before, we went to bed far from certain of being able to take off in the morning. As we journeyed from motel to Hartwood Field at dawn, the rains began and wetted down everyone's hopes. At the field, weather reports confirmed the visible. We sat around the hangar drinking coffee and hoping for a change, but instead of bettering, the elements wors-

Landing in power lines can be fatal, but once again, Forbes was lucky. The balloon was repaired in 24 hours for the final flight.

ened. By ten o'clock it was indisputably No Go.

The next day's forecast was at best problematical. Weather remains one of the many things one can do nothing about in ballooning. So we phoned to Fredericksburg and once more checked into the familiar surroundings of a Holiday Inn. With the *Capitalist Tool* at hand and New York not too far away, I flew back to the city, figuring in the afternoon and evening to make a slight dent in the office accumulation of Things to Be Done.

Late that night weather reports were far more encouraging and I set the alarm for 5:00 A.M. Morning brought clear skies in Virginia and high winds blowing from the west, so by 9:30 the *Tool* and I were back at Hartwood Field. Ground winds blew strong, so Dick Keuser had directed that the balloon be laid out at a low spot on the other side of the landing field, shielded by a forest of pines. There was a crowd on hand because it was clearly a Go morning.

Some days previously it was agreed Bobby would be aboard with his camera for the final day. For weeks he had relentlessly carried out the job that he and Tim, our youngest son, along with their lifetime friend John Ehrenclou had undertaken from the outset—to film the trip and tape the sounds that would make a documentary of a unique voyage. They had made movies from the bus, from the Crummies, the helicopter, the plane; they filmed takeoffs and landings; tenting, in motels, they filmed everywhere from every angle. All of us involved had learned to live with microphones thrust in front of us, with cameras clicking, and movies moving. It seemed only right that on the final day Bob should be aboard the balloon itself. At the time this was decided I had no idea that the last day's journey would prove to be so tense, dangerous, and at the end quite nearly, for me, really the end.

From the beginning we had referred to that distant time of completion as "the splashdown," a term borrowed from the astronauts, whose accomplishments in space somewhat dwarfed our voyage so close to earth and across such a small part of it. That morning, in going over final plans for takeoff and landing, I said two or three times that I would no longer refer

to the end of this day's trip as a splashdown. "If there is any possible way to avoid it we won't land in the water. It would be foolish to ruin or lose the things that have traveled all this way." I didn't want to spoil Bob's film nor dunk the mails we had carried the whole journey. "When we are near the Atlantic's edge, we'll set down on the land," said I with a final-decision tone of voice, and total intent.

Landing a balloon in water is a tricky business. With no wind, you can touch down on a water surface and keep your balloon inflated until a rescue vessel comes alongside. Things and people can then tidely be put aboard with few problems. But this day's conditions were far from the best. Surface winds were high and the waters near freezing. In a balloon if you hit water at a high speed, you must plan to bail out almost instantaneously with the impact; otherwise the gondola is likely to "submarine" and pin its occupants inside.

As you can see from the map, this last day's flight promised to be over water much of the time. There was the Potomac, the Rappahannock, the James and the wide expanse of Chesapeake Bay. Beyond the narrow band of land making the Chesapeake's eastern border was the Atlantic Ocean itself, a cold spread of water that I had no desire to taste.

On board were the two inflatable life vests that we had worn at takeoff in Coos Bay. (On that occasion we had known the wind was going to carry us first out over the Pacific, but the forecast of winds aloft had shown that at about 9,000 feet we should drift back over the Oregon coast and on northward and inland. Mae Wests were taken along because even the most casual reader of weather forecasts knows sometimes predictions don't turn out to be exact.) Having made sure the previous day that the air cylinders for instant inflation were intact and ready, I put them aboard. The final Winds Aloft report indicated the flight should be directly east, although at Hartwood Field the winds were blowing southeast. Since the ground winds were very high, I planned to leave "hot," i.e., many hands would hold the balloon down while it was heated to the point where it would bound into the air so fast that no wind sheer at tree level

Marking progress across the continent on the Magazine's Balloon Ascension Division bus. That day: 416 miles, unofficially exceeding the world record by more than 100 miles.

would carry us into obstacles nearby. The winds were predicted to be fast and out of the west at 10,000 to 12,000 feet, so I planned to go straight up there. Near the coast I would come down to a hundred feet above the water, blow across the Chesapeake, and land at the first good spot on the narrow peninsula between bay and ocean.

There was only one potential hazard that, in view of the predicted winds, seemed minimal. "You see," I said to Bob and the ground crew, "that opening between Norfolk and Cape Charles? It's 21 miles across and we don't plan to go thataway. We are going to keep our feet and Bob's film dry. There is going to be no splashdown," I concluded with all the authority of a transcontinental balloonist.

On that positive note we trucked on down to the balloon in the valley and started what turned out to be the most blustery inflation of the whole trip. The winds shifted so much so fast it took some doing to keep the inflating flames from burning parts of the balloon. It was clear we were going to have what an uninvolved observer might term an interesting takeoff.

There was a spooky, abandoned old house not far from the spot, and as the balloon finally filled and wildly waved about, we decided to move past that obstacle to the center of the field. It took all our experienced crew to keep the *Balleroy* under control. In the clear, and with All Hands firmly hanging on, I heated and heated until the pyrometer showed 180 degrees. At the signal they let go, and Bob and I literally bounded straight into the air.

As we neared 6,000 feet in less time than it had ever taken before, I noticed that the skirt was flapping wildly and that the wind seemed to be coming from several directions at once. Within two or three minutes we were in whispy clouds at 8,000 feet and the basket was shaking, swaying and jerking so that it was necessary to hang onto the rails. Although both flames were on high, for the first time in my ballooning experience they were blown out at the same instant. In the turbulence there was nothing that could be done about it. With no fire, the balloon cooled and descended to where the air was calmer, and it was easy to relight the fires and level off. We cruised at 5,000 feet

America from Coast to Coast · 47

for twenty or thirty minutes of calm flight and high speed.

The direction, though, wasn't as predicted. We were proceeding straight down the Rappahannock and toward that gap between Norfolk and Cape Charles that had been joked about before takeoff. It was still many miles away and there seemed lots of time to try finding winds at different altitudes which would bring us either south of Norfolk or toward Ocean City, Maryland. I went down to 1,000 feet, where the speed slowed to about eight knots. But no change of direction. So up we went to see if that west wind was to be found higher. No change at 10,000 feet or 12,000 feet or 14,000 feet or 15,000 feet.

While I was busy flying the balloon and navigating, Bob was having a field day. He'd already used one 400-foot roll of film at the takeoff, the excitement of which didn't seem to ruffle him at all. And certainly never distracted him from his picture taking. The Associated Press had asked him to take along one of their cameras to snap some stills for them, and he was doing that between filming. Every once in a while he would stick his right arm all the way out over the edge of the basket with camera in hand and snap a picture. "I might as well include myself in a couple of these, Pop, for the scrapbook," he explained. When we were banging around in the early turbulence and the flames had blown out, Bob didn't seem at all concerned. I figured he'd not done enough ballooning to realize that these were untoward events, not everyday occurrences. At any rate, his concentration on his job was total. This was his first and only day to photograph from the balloon, and nothing was going to—nor did, I might add—deter him from the mission.

Meanwhile, the prospect of a dry landing was coming more and more into doubt. Every few miles I'd plot the course line and it barely varied from our heading toward that gap that had seemed so small a part of the map when we took off. The *Capitalist Tool*, too, was plotting our course and their confirmation of my own plotting provided very little cheer.

As we neared the point where the Rappahannock empties into the Chesapeake, I realized

the time of decision, if we were to have a dry landing, was at hand. I made a final few rapid altitude changes to see if there was any change of direction. There wasn't and the captain of the *Tool* radioed that his latest Winds Aloft Forecast indicated little deviation.

I turned to Bob and said, "We're going down. Coming up is the only dry land between us and the Atlantic Ocean." His face expressed his disappointment that we were not to land literally on the coast line. With half a smile, he allowed as how he would prefer to have his film dry than to find out how it would weather a salt water dumping of uncertain duration. I advised both the *Tool* and the helicopter that we were going to try for Gwynn Island, the last bit of earth available before the bay and ocean. The two of us rapidly shed heavy jackets and put on the Mae Wests. I secured the radio and instrument panel and turned the ditty bag full of charts, maps, rations and wrenches from outside the gondola into it, and Bob wrapped the one complete film and the AP camera between Styrofoam layers inside a corrugated box brought for the purpose.

Venting and heating to establish a glide pattern onto Gwynn Island, we began to descend. The island came rapidly closer, but instead of looking larger it seemed even tinier than it had from higher up.

We were moving at a speed of about 25 knots and there was little by way of clearing to choose

Every few miles I'd plot the course line, and it barely varied from our heading toward that gap which had seemed so small a part of the map when we took off.

from on our flight path. There was a very small field bordered by a clump of trees, but the inevitable power lines were stretched right across the only possible landing spot. Just beyond them were several sheds of a small shipyard and then the rough wood dock of some fishermen. It quickly was obvious that, if we proceeded with this landing, we would for the second time in two days be tangled in power lines. That held no appeal. I quickly decided that our landing would be a wet one rather than a hot one.

It was one thing, though, to make that decision, and another to do it. While our glide pattern would have done a power plane pilot proud, changing it was not as simple as gunning power engines. I started blasting, and, as always in these circumstances, it seemed long minutes before the new heat slowed the descent, and even longer before it provided any lift. Bob was filming away while I bellowed at him to get down and for heaven sakes to stow that camera. It was a close one, but this time close in our favor. We just cleared that line and the trees behind it, and skimmed over the shipyard roofs on out across the bay.

There were still choices open to us. Beyond the island about two miles away were two or three tiny sand strips visible in the murky water and we were being blown toward them. There was no way to set down on one without dragging into water, but they did offer a slim chance of keeping both the balloon and us from total immersion. The other choice, since we were over the water headed for a wetting anyway, was to continue across the bay with a slim hope that the wind might just carry us to the fingers of Cape Charles rather than into the Atlantic.

After clearing Gwynn Island, we had passed over crabbing skiffs, but looking out across that wide bay, no other boats were in sight. I decided that those tiny dunes offered a much better prospect than the cold and empty ocean.

We were scudding along about 50 feet above the water. The surface was foam-streaked from the 25-knot winds. When hitting we'd be dragged under almost instantly. Quickly I reminded Bob, still filming—that nut—of the drill: Over the side a moment before impact.

Seconds later I grabbed the rip cord and shouted at Bobby, "Out!" Incredibly, he was still grinding that damned camera.

Then we hit. Plunging into the water, I lost both my glasses and grip on the red rip cord. With our weight out, the basket began to emerge from beneath the water. I struggled to get my right arm over the edge and reach that red cord, realizing that unless the top was swiftly ripped open the balloon and basket would float away.

From the moment of going over the side to the desperate struggle to hang onto the gondola and reach the red line, I had swallowed a bit of sea water with every gasp. As the gondola slowly rose, my numbing fingers slid down the edge of the basket and I started sinking again into the icy water. For the next few long-brief moments I thought I was going to drown. It would take too long to untie my heavy boots so I could swim. During those seconds of certainty of death I felt no terror, rather more a feeling of wry ruefulness—what a way to go.

Then the two miracles in my life happened.

As I flayed about in the water wondering when that kaleidoscopic review of my life would start as it's supposed to in a drowning, I saw Robert a dozen yards away walking—yes, walking—and from my salty-eyed, glassless perspective, he was walking on water.

Bob's potential ability to do this had been the subject of much joking within the family. In recent years he had grown a golden faceful of whiskers and shoulder-length hair. He looked for all the world like every Catechism picture of Christ Himself. We were so struck with the likeness that it had become a standing joke to say about his European trips that he should save the fare and walk across the Atlantic.

So you see it wasn't a total shock in my expiring moments to see Bob on foot on water.

But before I had time to figure out if I was already in Heaven or having a last look before descending into the Permanent Hot Place, the miracle evaporated. With a loud earthly voice 5b suggested that I stand up and stop trying to swim. Lo, the second miracle—this one for real: The water was not quite shoulder deep!

We waded ,shiveringly and gingerly toward

Tim Forbes in the chase helicopter caught the Chesapeake splashdown and rescue.

each other. As his welcome face became clearer to my unspectacled eyes, guess what also came inevitably into view—on his shoulder, that heavy camera. After happily assuring ourselves that we were each alive, relatively well, and rapidly freezing, we started toward a sand dune not too far away. I kept cautioning him to move carefully, that we might step right off the bar into the deep drink.

While we proceeded slowly and ever more numbly, our helicopter, the *Tool*, the NBC plane and a couple of other press planes kept circling overhead, flying by in low, slow passes, having a field day taking pictures. No boat appeared and I muttered darkly to Bob, "I don't suppose it's occurred to any of those bastards that it is cold down here. Can't they at least try to send one of those fishing skiffs our way?" Tim was happily filming from the helicopter. He'd shot the splashdown, then our water struggle and then the balloon's short solo flight and its descent. Finally he let the chopper hover over the nearest crabbing boat and direct it to us. In about a quarter of an hour, it putt-

putted alongside. Its captain, crew and owner were one person, Philip Smith. He helped us aboard and set out on the twenty-five-minute trip back to Gwynn Island. Our helicopter was already there and pilot Hughes arranged for a large fishing boat with four strong crewmen to go with him and retrieve the *Chateau de Balleroy*. As we drew up to the dock, there was Tim filming away. His first expression of concern was for the condition of Bob's film. We were pretty thoroughly chilled and the friendly new operators of the boat basin—refugees from Madison Avenue—took us into their nearby huge shore-style home. Both families—the Bergmans and the Nivens—were just in the process of moving in.

They filled a huge old-fashioned tub on the second floor into which I gladly sank, and another on the first floor into which Bob did likewise. As we sat and soaked they fed us hot soup and later coffee. By the time we emerged and put on borrowed sweaters, sweatpants and socks, the NBC crew had arrived on the scene to take a final shot.

Now, Jack Perkins is a brilliant TV reporter and a goodly part of his genius shows in the

fresh angles he takes on the events he films and in the wit and wryness of his commentary. I appreciated neither, though, when he began by asking, "Malcolm, are you going to finish the trip—or do you consider this the end?"

Because his crew was filming the answer, I smiled through my anger and declared that indeed this was the end. "We planned to go from sea to shining sea, and we've done so. The way the wind was blowing us, there was nothing between where we now sit and the Atlantic Ocean. As far as I'm concerned, we've completed our voyage across the United States."

"So you proclaim Gwynn Island the East Coast?" he murmured into the mike.

"Yes. In my book it is."

—Malcolm Forbes

3

CHAPTER

Ballooning
the Atlantic

Dick and Donna Brown

For some time, Forbes had set his sights on conquering the Atlantic by balloon. In March 1974 he consulted Dr. Thomas Heinsheimer, a distinguished aerospace scientist, who had an unequalled background in unmanned transatlantic flights with Mylar balloons. Heinsheimer, deep down, also had that growing urge to attempt a manned flight across the Atlantic.

Dr. Heinsheimer had been launching instrumented balloon systems for the past ten years but only recently started personally following his experiments into the atmosphere. He had been awarded an Advanced Scientific Research Fellowship by NATO and had been invited to join the scientific staff of the Service d'Aeronomie, the key French laboratory performing atmospheric research. He had worked on the Mercury and Apollo space programs, and in 1968 he joined the Aerospace Corporation in El Segundo, California. In July 1974 he took an extended leave of absence in order to devote his full attention to *Forbes* magazine's Atlantic Project. The entire technical effort leading to the design, production and tests of the balloon system and gondola were guided by Dr. Heinsheimer in his capacity as Program Director.

Forbes and Heinsheimer elected to follow some of the features of the ill-fated Gatch attempt, using high-flying clusters to ride the jetstream, thus avoiding the Atlantic weather at lower altitudes. They turned to Raven Industries of Sioux Falls, South Dakota, for the balloons and to major aerospace industries for the most modern technology available; namely, RCA Global Communications, Rockwell International, and Garrett Corporation.

A cluster of thirteen spherical superpressure balloons, each nearly 33 feet in diameter when fully inflated, were designed and constructed by Raven. The cluster design was unique—a 600-foot string of four tiers, each with three balloons, and a thirteenth balloon, inflated to a pressure 5 percent higher than the others, at the top to serve as a safety sentinel. Should *Windborne* ascend too high, the lead balloon would burst and the resultant loss of lift would drop the skyship to a safer altitude.

Tom Gatch used ten balloons in a single clus-

54 · Around the World on Hot Air & Two Wheels

* From *Ballooning* magazine, Spring 1975.

ter for his *Light Heart*. Communications with Gatch were lost on his second day out and although his balloon flotilla was sighted three days later, Tom Gatch was never seen nor heard from again. Hope that he will be found has dwindled with the passing of time. But Gatch was not the first aeronaut to fly clustered balloons. Back in 1957 Don Piccard flew the first flotilla, using twelve hydrogen balloons. At the time, Piccard was worried that the balloons rubbing against each other would build up a static charge and possibly set off an explosion.

But the Raven balloons for *Forbes* magazine's Atlantic Project were helium-filled. It was felt that, with a multiple balloon cluster, two or three balloons could malfunction without degradation of the flight profile. Each balloon was fitted with a load suspension harness for coupling to the main tether line. Each was equipped with a sensor for remote monitoring of its pressure.

The load suspension and rigging work for the Forbes Project was accomplished by Irvin Industries, Inc., of Gardena, California. The Irvin crew spent several days and nights in the old airship hangar at Santa Ana constructing and testing *Windborne*'s rigging. The lines were tested for six hours, testing each of the thirteen lines twenty times. The suspension harness as a whole was pull-tested to over 1½ times the weight of the payload. Irvin also installed individual chest-type parachutes for the crew in case of an emergency.

Windborne's balloons were superpressure balloons designed for constant altitude flight. They were made of high-strength polyester plastic film which is a tri-lamination consisting of three layers with a total thickness of .005 inch. Three balloons identical to *Windborne*'s were test-flown from the French Space Center in French Guiana.

The flotilla's payload was a spherical gondola with its precious human cargo. The distinctive craft was built by Neushul Corporation of Gardena, California, specialists in aircraft-oriented container systems. It had a 95-inch outside di-

Had all gone well, the Windborne *would have flown from California to Europe . . . and farther.*

Forbes inside the gondola mock-up, used for placement configuration.

ameter, 75 inches of standing room, eight portholes, and two hatches. It was a perfect aluminum sphere, with .025-inch thick walls covered with 2.4 inches of foam insulation and a thin aluminized plastic film.

According to the gondola's structural designer, Dr. Leonard Hart-Smith, a spherical shape was selected because it is the most efficient means of containing the interior atmosphere. Despite the thin skin, the load stresses are so low that the riveted and bonded shell could withstand over eight times the pressure anticipated in flight.

A 14-inch-wide mast in the center of the gondola provided structural integrity to the aluminum sphere and central housing for all major operational systems. These systems included lithium batteries for power, fans for air circulation, lithium hydroxide for carbon dioxide removal, molecular sieve for moisture removal, electrical control panel, and electronics for communications, telemetry and navigation.

Ballooning the Atlantic · 55

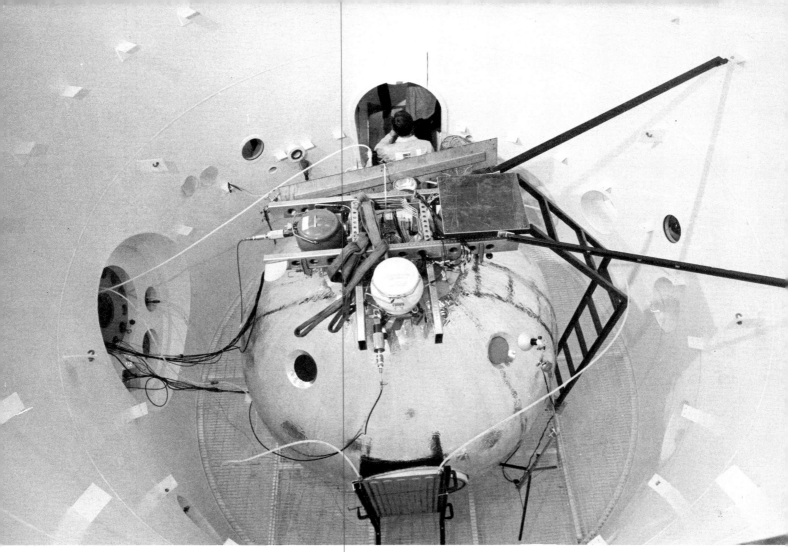

The completed gondola is readied for an altitude test inside an atmospheric pressure tank at Rockwell Industries.

Outside, on the top of the gondola, which was designed to float, there were several crossbars to which the balloons were attached. Also mounted on the crossbars were tanks of liquid oxygen and nitrogen (the aeronauts would live in a 45- to 50-percent oxygen environment) and various communications antennas. Also there was a winch with a 500-foot weighted dragline.

Should an emergency develop in flight and it become necessary to abandon ship, the crew were prepared to egress from one of *Windborne*'s hatches. They were advised not to leave the gondola if above 28,000 feet because of severe physiological problems. However, they were briefed on breathing techniques without a bailout oxygen supply if they did have to egress at altitudes above 28,000 feet. Long-delay free falls were discouraged owing to "spin-up" and chill-factor problems. Malcolm and his copilot were instructed on the use of the chest parachutes and exiting backwards through the hatch.

Windborne's communications systems bordered on the sophistication of NASA's space shots. Technical data and flight status reports in the form of numerically coded messages were to be relayed from *Windborne* via NOAA's Synchronous Meteorological Satellite to the satellite ground station at Wallops Island, Virginia, then to the NOAA computer for further transmittal by teletype to RCA's Globcom headquarters. Position, environmental and subsystem data would come from the six Navy Transit satellites that circle the earth every 90 minutes.

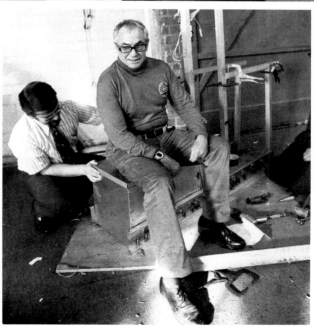

(TOP) *Discussing launch procedures;* (MIDDLE LEFT) *communications are tried out before the high-altitude pressure test;* (RIGHT, BOTTOM) *a seat is fitted, wiring checked.*

Ballooning the Atlantic · 57

A vital part of Forbes's Atlantic Project was the Mission Control Center set up at an RCA New York facility. The MCC was to maintain a continuous monitor of flight performance and vital communications including voice channels by VHF aeronautical radio and HF maritime/aeronautical radio. Monitoring on the ocean's other side was to be performed by the French Space Agency at Toulouse, France. Forbes's own DC-9 "chase plane" would serve as a mobile flight operations center and a communication link in the air-tracking operations and possibly in the rescue operations.

Fly across the Atlantic starting from California? Yes, the mission flight plan was to climb to 40,000 feet and ride the jet stream across the continent as a trial run, estimated to last between twenty-four and forty-eight hours. During this evaluation period, all systems would be checked out prior to a commitment for an Atlantic crossing. If it was a "go" situation, the skyship would proceed and hopefully land in eastern Europe or northern Africa in four to seven days. If problems occurred, the mission

director would declare a "no-go" situation and a landing would be attempted in the United States. At that time the aeronauts would don their restraint harnesses and parachute helmets and proceed with a controlled descent and eventual impact on the ground.

With its vertical extent of over 1,000 feet, Dr. Heinsheimer likened *Windborne* to a flying weather tower. Inserted in the jet stream, the skyship would drift freely with the wind, causing a minimum of atmospheric perturbations by its presence. Thus, *Windborne* would become a novel way to make scientific measurements along a vertical profile. There were ten major atmospheric experiments housed within the gondola, on the crossbars, within the balloons, and along the length of dragline.

A few days before the launch, a twenty-one-man crew performed a practice launch using small helium balloons, the specially designed winch carts, and the *Windborne* gondola itself. The procession wheeled the system down the 1,000-foot length of Hangar One and out the giant doors to the launch pad. Under the guidance of Launch Director Jean Pierre Pommereau, the crew practiced the deployment of balloon clusters and rectified several problems of tangling and twisting.

The actual launch had been delayed several

Rolling out for final countdown.

but by 10 o'clock that evening, the meteorologists predicted that the winds would be favorable by 3 o'clock Monday morning. It was January 6 and for *Windborne* it was finally "GO."

Hangar One became a scene of bustling activity as *Windborne* and her entourage of silvery balloons proceeded out the hangar door and into the chilly Pacific air. Sealed within the gondola were aeronauts Malcolm Forbes, Tom Heinsheimer and Tlalos, a miniature representation of the Mexican God of the Wind.

The lead balloon and first cluster were raised with no problem. As the second cluster was being raised, the release mechanism slipped and the cluster shot abruptly into the air. With instant reflexes, the ground crew jumped on the third cluster's cart to prevent a chain reaction. It was 4:00 A.M. and a hold was announced while the crew assessed their situation. At this time, the ground breezes were on a slight increase. There was an air of apprehension as four large searchlights, one aimed at each balloon cluster, plus several banks of floodlights, cast an eerie glow across the launch site. A host of fellow aeronauts and special guests huddled near the lights for warmth, anxious to see *Windborne* get off the ground so that they could return to a warmer place to monitor the skyship's aerial progress.

For nearly an hour *Windborne* sat on the launch pad with its lead balloon and top two tiers already waving in the breeze. Then, suddenly, a gust caused the remaining two clusters to drag their weighted carts! To the horror of the spectators and ground handlers, the balloons clattered and banged into each other as they tore away from their moorings! Jean Pierre jumped onto the top of the tumbling gondola and without a second to spare cut the balloons

As the balloon clusters are slowly let up into the vertical configuration (LEFT), a release control ring snaps and the cluster jerks upward (RIGHT).

times because of weather conditions. The New Year 1975 blew in so briskly that it caused power outages in the Santa Ana area. January 1 settled in as a very blustery day. The launch was postponed and rescheduled tentatively for the upcoming weekend. By Saturday it was apparent that the delay needed to be extended another day. That evening the Goodyear blimp *Columbia* circled Hangar One with the following message flashing across its night sign: "The U.S. Marine Corps and Goodyear Wish the Best of Luck to the Transatlantic Balloon Flight." Another postponement came Sunday morning,

The disabled gondola just after Forbes and Heinsheimer were rescued. Its violent rolling on the ground came close to exploding the liquid oxygen tanks on top.

With the gondola's exterior systems smashed, quick-thinking Launch Director Jean-Pierre Pommereau released the balloons, sending them aloft.

free! While searchlights played on the soaring clusters, the crowd surged forward. Immediately the aeronauts unbuckled their safety harnesses, opened the hatch, and escaped without injury. The area was quickly evacuated for fear that the liquid oxygen tanks might rupture.

Immediately after the mishap, Forbes credited Jean Pierre with saving the pilots' lives. At great danger to himself, he had activated the emergency quick disconnect which cut the balloons from the gondola. If the launch had not been aborted, the capsule would have been severely damaged and perhaps lifted in that condition into the stratosphere. Undaunted, and with tremendous enthusiasm, Forbes announced that he and Dr. Heinsheimer would try again.

Mission Director Donald R. Scheller described what happened during the launch attempt: "The balloons, flying free of the gondola weight, climbed rapidly above their design flight altitude and one by one failed because of overpressure until the dead weight of the burst balloons and harness exceeded the lifting capacity of the remaining intact balloons. At this point, the system descended slowly until approximately 8:30 A.M. (PST) when it landed in Henderson Canyon in Anza Borrego Desert State Park, California. There, the trailing burst balloons snagged on the rocky terrain holding it fast until secured by Park Rangers. The balloons were tracked by aircraft visual sightings and by NORAD radar. The Los Angeles Air Route Traffic Control Center used the data to provide safe air traffic control separation to aircraft."

Scheller added, "The Forbes Magazine's Atlantic Project personnel wish to take this opportunity to express their deepest appreciation and sincere thanks for the outstanding support provided by the multitude of people and organizations who so generously and effectively assisted in this endeavor. Some of these who contributed so greatly are: the U.S. Marine Corps and its personnel at the Marine Corps Helicopter Station, Santa Ana, California; the U.S. Air Force Aerospace Rescue and Recovery Service, MAC, Scott Air Force Base and its subordinate units; Headquarters U.S. Air Force Operations Center personnel; the U.S. Coast

After the nearly fatal launch, a distraught wife . . .

Guard and its RCC at Governor's Island, New York City; the Federal Aviation Administration and its System Command Center and Los Angeles ARTTC personnel; ARINC, AVMETS, the Navy Astronautics Group at Point Mugu, California; the National Oceanographic and Atmospheric Agency, Suitland, Maryland, and Wallops Island, Virginia; NASA, Goddard Space Flight Center; the French Government's Space and Research Agencies CNES and CNRS; RCA Globcom, New York; and the aviation departments of Spain, Portugal, Morocco, Senegal, Mauritania, Mali, and France; and all others not specifically mentioned."

A few days after the aborted launch, the pilots reported that *Windborne*'s 13-balloon system appeared to be too complicated and that the balloon configuration would be re-examined and probably redesigned. It would be months before another flight could be attempted. Had they been successful, they would have set two new records in ballooning; the duration record of 87 hours set in 1913 and the distance record of 1,896 miles set in 1914. More importantly, had they been able to keep their date with the jet stream, Malcolm Forbes and Tom Heinsheimer would have been the first to cross the Atlantic by balloon.

Explaining to the press what went wrong. Instead of a flight to glory, crushing disappointment; but, at least, instead of tragedy, the chance to balloon some more.

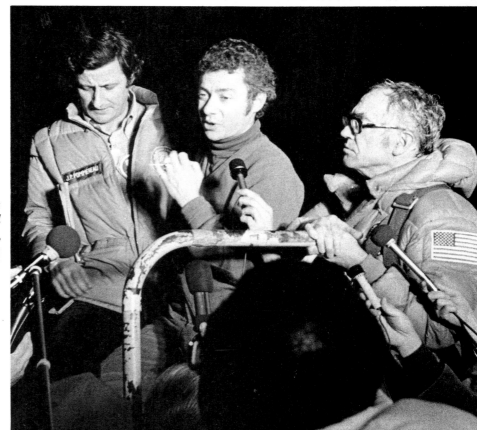

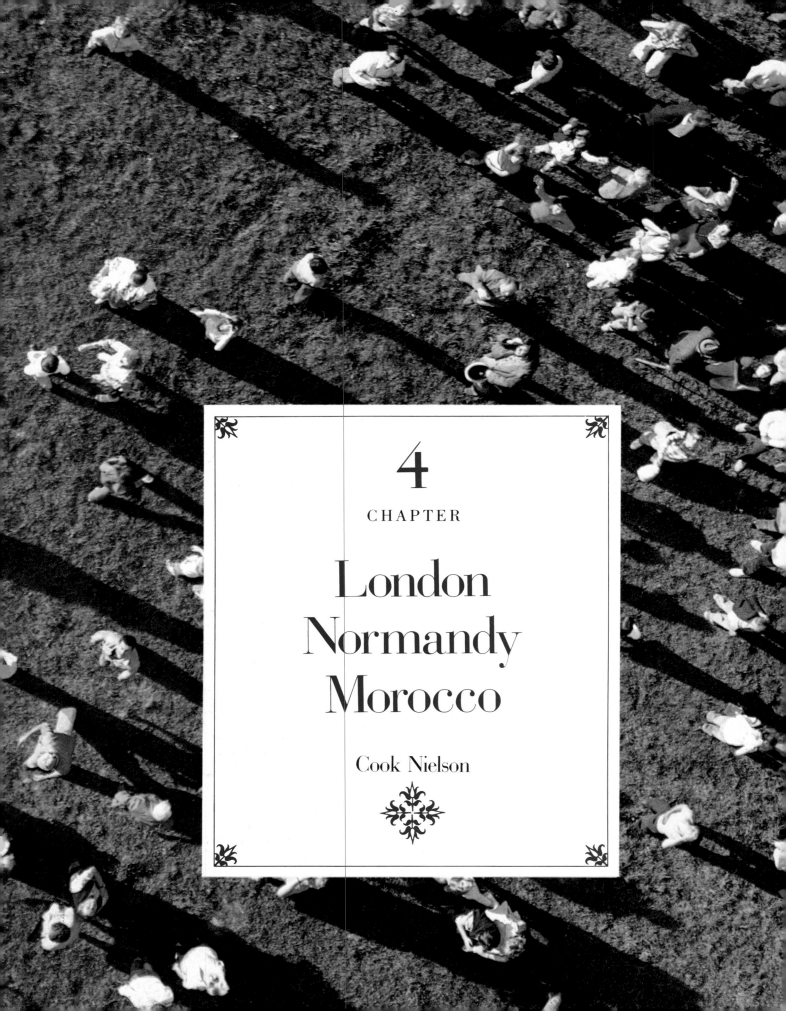

CHAPTER

4

London
Normandy
Morocco

Cook Nielson

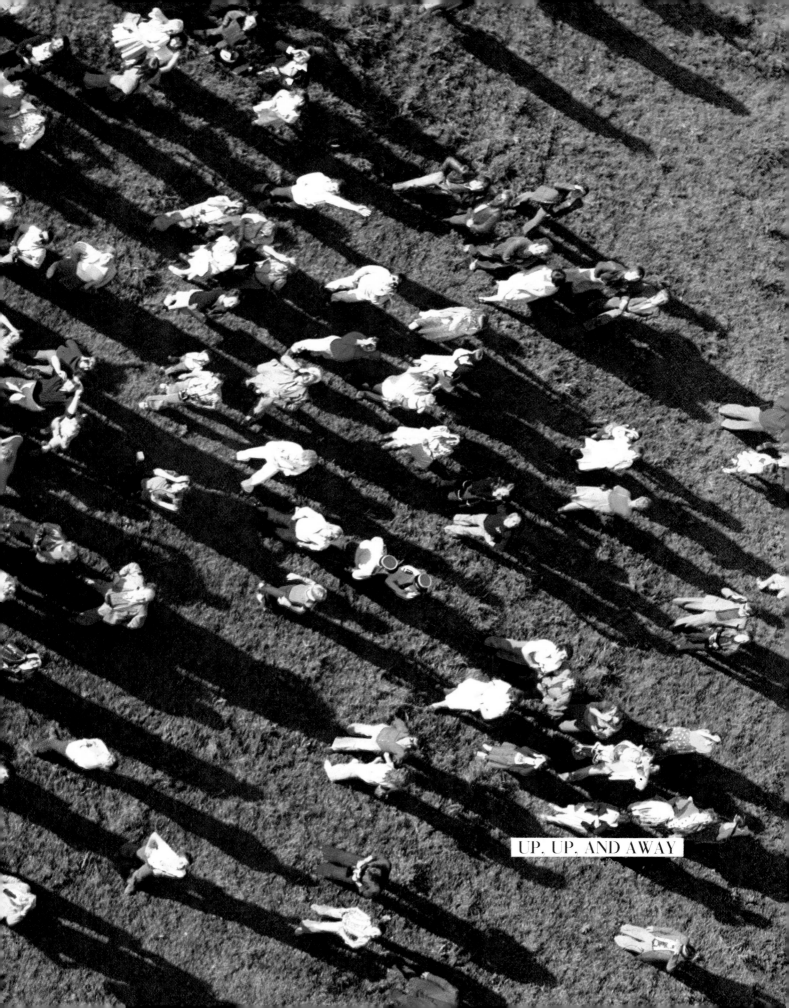

UP, UP, AND AWAY

J une 8, 1978: Today the trip begins, and if ever a motorcycle tour were to depend on good luck and the kindness of strangers, this is it. I am not particularly worried about the Honda GL— it is sound, and it is a Honda. But there are no tools and no spares for the Harley, and while the Van Veen carries a positively BMW-esque toolkit, there is no manual to speak of and none of us knows a single thing about it except where to put the gas and oil. Only Malcolm, Bob and I will travel this first leg of the journey. Kip Cleland, the director of Forbes's Physical Fitness Program, is waiting to join us in Normandy.

Leaving early in sharp British sunshine, we battle through the morning traffic of London suburbs and, immediately lost, try to head in the general direction of Ramsgate, where we will catch the Hovercraft across the English Channel to Calais. Although there are

The machines we used represent some of motorcycling's thoroughbreds.

many distractions—where we are or are not, crosswalk protocol, riding on the wrong side of the road, this very strange swaying Van Veen— I study Malcolm the rider.

He is damn good. Accurate, capable and a bit of a thruster, Malcolm handfights his way toward Ramsgate, stopping only when absolutely necessary to consult the map. We are not exactly trickling down the road, either. Malcolm's favorite pace is "brisk," and he humps the Hog with authority and some style, gouts of oil smoke puffing from the Harley's tailpipe in quantities large enough to smell whenever we come to a stop sign. He knows what he's doing, and one of my main concerns— headlines in *The New York Times* announcing: "Famous Business Magazine Owner Skragged on Bike While Traveling with Cycle Magazine Twit"—begins to melt away.

We get to Ramsgate just in time to see our Hovercraft swell up like a

The Hovercraft provided a bouncier ride than the bikes.

frightened blowfish and slip heavily into the Channel on its way to France. No matter. We will catch the next one. The Hovercraft ferry looks and acts like a Rube Goldberg cartoon come to life and gone bananas. It uses turbine engines to create the cushion of air upon which it floats, and any number of propellers on pivoting stalks for propulsion and aim. It is thought of by those who run it as an aircraft. There are stewardesses on board, and the trips are called "flights."

When we wheel the bikes into the hold we are requested to put them on their center stands. Malcolm looks studiously for such a device on the Harley before discerning that there is none. "My technical knowledge of motorcycles is zilch," he says. "If I press the starter and it doesn't start, sometimes I remember to turn the off button to on and sometimes I don't, and sometimes I remember to turn the petcock on, and sometimes I don't."

The "flight" took about forty-five minutes. We went through customs in Calais and headed for the Chateau de Balleroy through some of the most beautiful country in the civilized world. That afternoon I give the Van Veen its head on the autoroute (France's version of the autobahn) and watch the speedometer needle achieve

the 225 kph mark (about 139.5 mph.). The wind strips my luggage off the seat.

The twin-rotor Van Veen is purely a creature of the open road. Its four-speed gearbox, chunky weight carried high, tall overall gearing, diabolical centerstand, grabby hydraulic clutch, heavy throttle springing and rotary engine surging conspire against elegant progress in traffic, but once away from all that, the bike becomes a delicacy. Its engine is the precise displacement equivalent of two Suzuki RE5s; only the Honda CBX and Yamaha XS Eleven are in its league for speed. The engine need not turn a lot of rpm to perform. Indeed, its 6500 rpm redline is not far above that of many domestic automotive V-8s. But the bike's cruising smoothness and mid-range throttle response, together with a decent seat and excellent riding position, give its rider the ability to absorb mammoth distances almost unconsciously.

Malcolm is pleased to hear this. Despite the fact that it was his $11,000 that bought the Van Veen, he has not ridden it, which causes me to feel like a living diorama.

We get to the Chateau de Balleroy at 8:30 P.M., but we know where it is before we can see it because Ed Yost's silver barrage balloon, tethered in a field behind the chateau, is visible from 15 or 20 kilometers away. We approach the main drive at a slant, turn left onto it, and momentarily are crunching through white gravel between maze-like formal hedge gardens and various outbuildings toward the stairway leading to the entrance.

The Forbes chateau is one of the most beautiful buildings in all of Europe. It is big—but not so big as to be the sort of building in which no one lives. There is a central section having what appear to be four stories, two flanking wings, and a pair of non-attached smaller buildings that from the front look like miniature versions of the central section. It was built by François Mansart between 1626 and 1636 for a man named Jean de Choisy, became the property in 1698 of Jacques de la Cour, and then stayed with a succession of Balleroys until purchased in 1970 by the Forbes Investors Advisory Institute.

Its charm is inescapable. Its proportions

make it seem smaller than it really is. The rooms inside are large, of course, but remodeling has made them warm.

We are greeted upon arrival by members of Malcolm's New York staff, members of his French staff, and representatives of his Balloon Ascension Division staff. We have covered some 600 kilometers today. The bikes so far are fine. We are in bed shortly after dinner. And where we are sleeping is a far cry from a KOA campground, or a ditch with a snake for company.

JUNE 9: I awaken at two in the afternoon and join Malcolm and his guests for lunch. Malcolm says, "I've been riding my motorcycle around in the moat for the past three hours hoping you'd take my picture." There is in fact a moat; a dog lives in it.

This is not your ordinary country weekend at the chateau. It is the weekend of the Fourth Annual International Balloon Meeting—Friday,

At the balloon meet in Normandy, France, held every June, Forbes hosts pilots and their colorful craft from around the world.

London/Normandy/Morocco · 69

(RIGHT) *Cook Neilson, Bob Forbes, and MSF prior to takeoff for Morocco.*

(*LEFT*) *One year, dropping hang gliders while aloft was a highlight.*

Saturday and Sunday—and it will host aeronauts from France, America, England, Ireland, Sweden, Holland, Belgium, Germany, Poland and Iran. There is the closest thing to a county fair thrown in for good measure: balloon rides (on the barrage balloon), a dog show, gymnastics exhibitions, all manner of diversions, eats and games.

Balloons of all shapes and sizes. When the weather's good the big bags of hot air drift off one by one, returning to the ground a while later for another flight.

Only half an hour from Balleroy are the Normandy beachheads and a major U.S. military cemetery; with Bayeux and the tapestry only 6 miles away, we are reminded how small the Channel can be.

In 1984, the fortieth anniversary of D-Day, many reenactments and remembrances were held at the sites.

After lunch Bobby and I ride the Honda and the Harley to the Normandy cemetery. There are 9,386 graves, and on a wall the names of an additional 1,557 missing. Despite the chilly symmetry of the gravestones it is a lovely place, situated atop a cliff overlooking Omaha Beach, the scene of the greatest amphibious troop landing in history. There are gardens of roses, stands of European Ash, beds of heather and boxwood. Afterwards we ride east to a museum where the artifacts and the technology of the landing are displayed, and then we hustle back to the chateau to get cleaned up for the aeronauts' banquet, at which Malcolm makes pre-

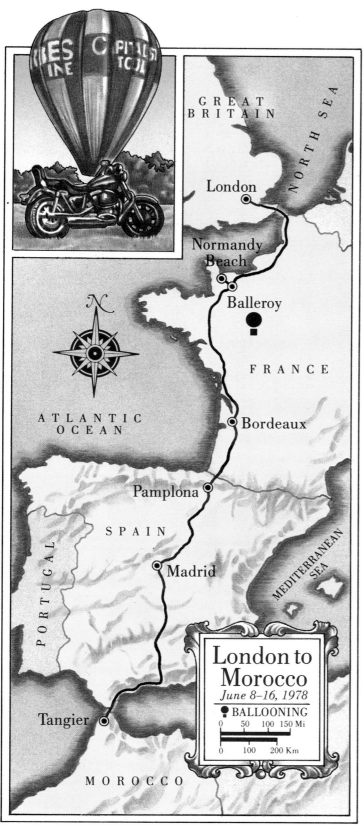

London to Morocco
June 8–16, 1978

● BALLOONING

0   50   100 150 Mi

0   100   200 Km

A converted stable on the chateau grounds holds the world's first balloon museum, where the history of this earliest form of aeronautics is displayed.

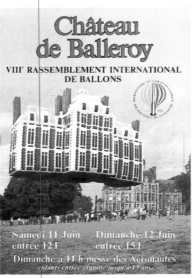

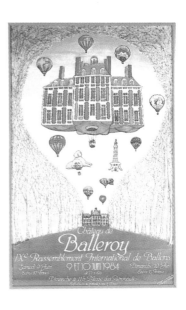

Kassia Leprieur, majordomo of the chateau, brings out the Coupe de Balleroy, given annually to the balloonists who have made the year's greatest contribution to the sport.

sentations to each of the balloon teams and welcomes them. I am seated between a lacquered lady from Chicago and British balloonist Royston Cooper, an amalgam of the Schlitz Malt Liquor bull and Groucho Marx who the next night will wear a linen napkin on his head as a helmet against corks ricocheting off the ceiling.

The award ceremony is a highlight of a festive weekend for people in the area. In 1979, the recipients were the first trio to balloon the Atlantic. Two have since died—Maxie Anderson in a balloon, Ben Abruzzo piloting a small plane.

Every year, a fireworks display set to music kicks off the weekend's celebration.

After dinner we walk around to the rear of the chateau. A thirty-minute fireworks display has been arranged. Music thunders out of two speakers as big as Buicks and glowing embers sift down through the forest flanking the field to the delight of some five thousand townspeople who had assembled quietly while we were eating. I ask Malcolm when he's going to show us

the main chateau. Malcolm chuckles. "Ahh," he says, "be it ever so humble . . . Well, everyone has to have a little something to call his own."

June 10: Late this afternoon I fly in Malcolm's balloon *Moira*. It is piloted by Sid Cutter, who is regarded, though not necessarily by Sid, as the best balloonist here. Flying in a balloon across the afternoon Normandy countryside is the farthest thing from a sobering experience. One moment the *Moira* is a long, thick red and yellow trunk of fabric resting on the green grass of the chateau meadow, attached to a wicker basket with a number of small-diameter filaments. The next it has been blown up with a large fan, the air within heated by tongues of flame blasting out of its basket-mounted propane burners, and is rising in serene and perfect stateliness from the meadow and the hundreds of people gathered below. We have become a puff of color; we have assumed the shape of whimsy.

There is, of course, no breeze to feel—we are at one with the air, we are in the air as palpably as a swimmer is in the water. We flow suspended and still across the top of France's soft gold-lit greenness hearing nothing except gentle barnyard noises from below, and from above the distant intermittent honk of other balloons' propane burners. We are waving at all the farmers and their children as we parade majestically overhead, and they, laughing and ecstatic, are waving back at us. Rabbits frightened by our shadow scamper down alfalfa rows; we can hear their feet. Cows let out from milking stare up and move around for a better view. "You know," Sid says, "there isn't anybody who doesn't love a balloon." It cuts through me like a knife; I am a motorcyclist, after all.

We have been up for forty-five minutes or an hour, and it is time to find a spot to land. There are priorities. A landing site should be near a road; there should be access to a road so our pickup crew can get to us easily; there should be no domestic animals nearby, especially horses, especially Thoroughbred horses (these have been known to entangle themselves in barbed wire fences at the sight of a balloon); the landing site should not be a crop field, nor too close to a fence; and there should be a windrow, forest or some other form of wind protection to make the landing as trauma-free as possible. Sid, naturally, finds just such a place. I

London/Normandy/Morocco · 79

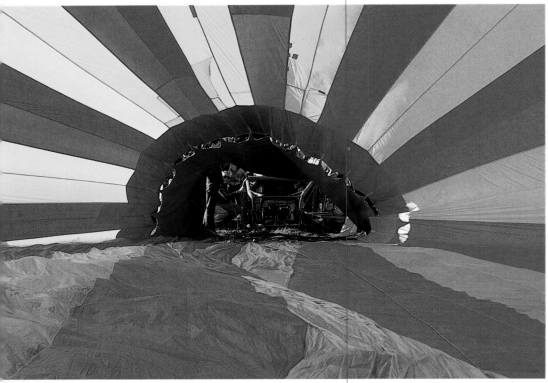

The Norman countryside paints a luxuriant backdrop for the many multicolored balloons; its farms provide plenty of soft spots for landings.

was told that ordinarily the population of the entire region rushes toward a balloon when it lands, to see what it's like, to meet whoever's in it, and to help secure the sizable bulk of the gas bag against the currents of the wind. Our landing is ordinary: forty or fifty people materialize from nowhere to lay hands on the gondola while Sid takes the top out of *Moira* and releases the heated air. The balloon collapses quietly and with dignity, is laid out and folded up, and twenty minutes later we have said our thank-yous and good-byes and are on our way back to the chateau in a van driven by Monsieur Garnier, the head of *Moira*'s chase crew.

That night Royston Cooper gives me a champagne shampoo at dinner to commemorate my first flight. While my head is still dripping and bubbling he tells me, "Everyone loves your hairdo. They say the Moët brings out the highlights."

JUNE 11: I fly again this afternoon, this time with Denny Fleck, the Manager of Forbes's Balloon Ascension Division. When we land it is just like yesterday. Everyone from the nearby town—children pink-cheeked and hot to practice their English, thick-armed friendly farmers, chattering womenfolk—surround the gondola and hold it firm while the bag comes down. "What is the word in English for *ballon*?" the children want to know. "It is balloooooon!" we tell them, again and again. "Balloooooooooon!"

JUNE 12: Today we leave for Morocco. Denny Fleck is up before us and has the bikes—the

After a full French country weekend, it's time to get back on the road to Morocco.

Van Veen, the Harley, and two GL1000s—warmed and ready to go. Kip Cleland will ride with Malcolm, Bobby and me. Despite Kip's superb condition the weekend at Balleroy has exacted a merciless toll, and to make matters worse he had dropped something heavy on his foot the night before and is therefore feeling discomfort from both ends.

It will be a long pull. Mary Ann Danner, Malcolm's executive secretary, has estimated the distance to be 600 km to Bordeaux, and when the day is done exactly 600 km have rolled up on the Harley's odometer. Our route takes us through Saint-Lô, Villedieu-les-Poêles, Rennes and Avranches before lunch in Nantes, a meal which prompts Malcolm to note that the frog's legs are underdone and the

salad was served before the soup, and then to be amused that a bunch of black-clad motorcyclists would dare complain about such things. The possibility hits me like a train that the French cuisine Malcolm enjoys at home is superior to anything we might find in France.

On after lunch, Kip now revived, to Rochelle, Saintes, then a kiss of cool, damp air as we pass close to the ocean at Saint-André-de-Cubzac, and finally into Bordeaux, where Bobby, using nets of fluent French, stalks and captures our hotel. It is the Aquitania, an ultramodern white hulk of a building far from what we all anticipated to be the viny charm of downtown Bordeaux.

Today's route has not been particularly scenic; Malcolm is not a sightseer. He is a straight-

On the road, directions are wherever you can find them.

ahead traveler, unlike other American tourists chiefly in that he is focused on a destination which is meaningful to him. We are but one day from the Chateau de Balleroy and already he has caught the scent of the Palais Mendoub, probably his favorite place of all. For motorcyclists what counts is the trip, not the objective. Malcolm cares about the trip but not because of what he sees. He cares about the trip because he gets to ride.

A distance beyond Mont Saint-Michel, Bobby had noticed a piece of paper fluttering from Malcolm's pocket. We stop. The green insurance card for the yellow GL turns up missing. Without it the bike might not be allowed into Spain. There is no question about alternatives: if we get hung up crossing the border Kip will ride the Honda back to the chateau, drop off the bike, go to Paris and fly to Morocco.

JUNE 13: We leave Bordeaux after attending to the fluid needs of the bikes, ride past a series of horrendous truck wrecks and arrive for lunch at the two-star Hôtel des Pyrénées in Saint-Jean-Pied-de-Port. During a perfectly stunning

luncheon Malcolm prepares Kip gently for the possibility of his having to return to the chateau: riding north through France, then flying from Paris to Tangier, we agree, is hardly an onerous task.

But the border is crossed without investigation or incident, and we spend the early after-

With four different registrations for the bikes, Customs isn't always amused.

noon indulging in the dips and twists of the road through the Pyrenees. Malcolm is every bit as steady in the mountains as he was in English rush-hour traffic, Bobby rides with supple lyricism, and Kip gets by with enthusiasm and blocky muscularity. I have Bob follow me for a time to show him what I think I know about lines, and then I track him to see what he's picked up. He has picked up everything and is grinding away at the Honda's foot pegs. "There's nothing more I can teach you," I tell him.

Evening finds us in Pamplona. As I ride the Harley down the ramp to the underground parking lot I notice it is sounding a little rough. No wonder—both header bolts have fallen out, and the exhaust system is held more or less in place by nothing but the muffler support. We have a long distance still to cover; a way must be found to secure the header pipes. I am overtaken by the feeling of grim determination touring riders speak of; the problem will be fixed.

Bobby and I clean up and then walk to the nearest hardware store, which is about to close. Using Bob's mixture of French and Italian and a series of sketches we buy several metric bolts in different lengths, taps to match, an adjustable wrench and handfuls of washers.

But the bolts are all too big—they won't fit through the holes in the exhaust flanges. Now it's time to think: Where in Pamplona at eight o'clock in the evening would we be able to find just the right American bolts? The answer was in front of us: the Harley. I spin out a likely looking bolt from the luggage rack and it fits perfectly through the exhaust flange and into the front head. One more transplant and we're off to dinner, and then to bed.

JUNE 14: Today's destination is Madrid. It's cool as we plow through Tuleda, Tarazona, Soria. The countryside is like the western U.S.: stark. Poverty is all around us and ancient religious buildings peer down from the tops of distant hilltops. We lunch in Medinaceli, then race rain clouds all the way to Tonja, just north of Guadalajara, where we break into the clear. It's an easy canter from there to Madrid. Malcolm had told us at lunch that our hotel is the Ville Magni. There is just enough left of the memory

Without a specific language, hands sometimes have to do the job. With varying results.

of what he said for me, suddenly and utterly lost by myself in teeming Madrid, to communicate the name to a taxi driver, whom I paid to lead me to our hotel. Malcolm had discussed this taxi technique the day before. Good thing. I doubt I would have been able to think of it myself, and without it I would have been in some serious trouble: not much money, no Spanish, the day almost gone, and lost beyond imagining.

A good ride is not one of arrow-straight superhigh-ways, but of roads with twists and turns. The quality of the roads, though, can sometimes be off-putting, as Cook found out in Spain.

JUNE 15: Around noon I crashed the yellow GL1000 on a humpy, polished little road 30 km north of Granada. I was riding third, behind Malcolm and Kip. The road is an old one, pounded by the heavy trucks traveling between Granada and Jaén. In each lane where the tires roll, there are channels. I got the front tire off-cambered against the flank of a rut, lost it, the bike sank down on the right-side engine guard, the back tire unloaded, and the bike went rooting and sparking across the road and into the weeds on the far side. Bobby just missed me. But almost before I had stopped sliding the reflex which must be common to all pro photographers had Bob clicking away.

It took three of us to hoist the GL back on the road. We were relieved to discover no serious damage—the engine guard, the corner of the fairing—and it fired right up as if nothing had happened at all.

Our original plans called for a stop in Granada, but by now Malcolm was aching for Tangier and the Palais Mendoub. Granada came and went, and by the time we got to Málaga, Malcolm had the Van Veen ("You can't beat it for passing") belly to the ground. We would spend the night in Algeciras and catch the first ferry to Tangier the next morning.

The fanciest hotel in Algeciras is the Reina Cristina, a lovely, regal place which looks across the bay at the Rock of Gibraltar. It was very late in the afternoon when we got there. We had no reservations. We were tired, dirty. We were motorcyclists. Malcolm got us rooms in two minutes flat.

JUNE 16: The Van Veen's throttle cable breaks as we mount up and head for the ferry. We are a bit late leaving the hotel anyway, and there is little time to lose. I whip out the Van Veen's tool roll, yank off the fuel tank and find that the bike has a pull-pull throttle cable arrangement. I connect the return cable to the opener slot in the butterfly pulley, attach its other end to the twist grip spool, leave the twist grip housing loose to accommodate the return cable's length, and we're in business.

The Van Veen makes it out the hotel driveway and stops dead in its tracks. It is out of fuel, and we don't know exactly where the dock is, and time is running out. We coast down a slope, looking for a gas station. What do we find? The dock.

But the situation continues to unravel. We fall prey to some sharpy who helps us buy tickets on the wrong ferry going to the wrong place, the bikes are parked in the wrong queue, the yellow GL—the one I crashed—conks out altogether from an electrical malfunction, we do not discover until almost too late that buying tickets is only the tip of the paperwork iceberg, and the loading boss is reluctant to converse with us in French even though it is probably his native tongue.

But still we make it, two dead bikes notwithstanding. Gas from the GL is beer-bottled into the Van Veen's tank during the trip across the Strait, and customs in Tangier is no problem because the customs boss knows Malcolm. We leave the GL under guard in a parking lot in the

We had no reservations. We were tired, dirty. We were motorcyclists. Malcolm got us rooms in two minutes flat.

A transfer of gas to an empty tank.

Tangier harbor and head for Rue Shakespeare and the Palais Mendoub. We are there in plenty of time for lunch, which is served under palm trees in the garden by two Moroccans.

You could call the palais a nice, big house: it would barely fit between the end zones of a football field. It contains a museum and was formerly the governor's palace. My room looks out

London/Normandy/Morocco · 87

The Palais Mendoub, a former royal palace and once the home of FORBES magazine's Arabic edition, now houses a toy-soldier collection. It draws more than 300 people a week.

Many rooms with views.

towards Gibraltar; the view from my bathroom takes in Tangier harbor. The trip is over.

The next few days pass quickly. I spend time exploring the palais. Both Kips (Kip Cleland and Kip Forbes, Malcolm's son), Mary Ann, Bob and I venture down to the Kasbah to haggle with the shopkeepers, I behave myself moderately well at a black tie party in honor of the Countess de Breteuil, and there is time to enjoy the pool and the sunshine and the luxurious breeze that bathes the palais from dawn to dusk. I have time to think about the trip, and all the people I have met; about crashing in Spain, and Harley header bolts, and Victorian art collections; about balloon rides, vintage wines, broken cables and the magic light of northern France.

I will wait for six months, I decide. A year at the longest. And then I will encourage Malcolm to write another touring story.

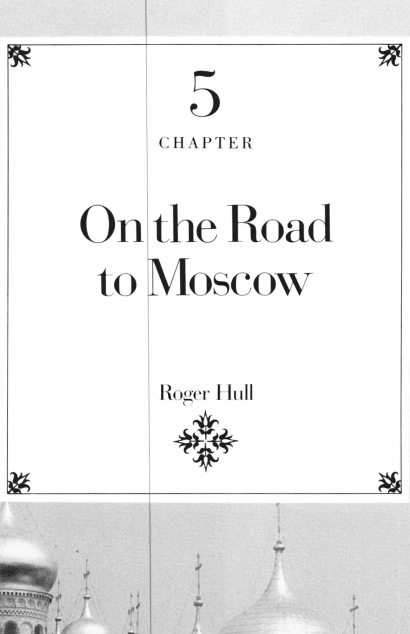

5

CHAPTER

On the Road to Moscow

Roger Hull

I

Once upon a time the Soviet government absolutely refused to issue visas to people who wanted to ride motorcycles through Russia. That was true right up until the late afternoon of Sunday, June 24, 1979, when they bent that rule a little and admitted six American motorcyclists who were en route to Moscow. I was privileged to be one of the six.

Plans for this history-making trek began nearly a year earlier when Malcolm Forbes invited me to be his guest for a midsummer motorcycle ride in Europe. Initially he was thinking in terms of France, West and East Germany and Poland; then back to London, maybe via Copenhagen. Shortly thereafter, however, his objective became Moscow. When Malcolm learned that visas simply were not issued to motorcyclists wishing to travel through Russia, it presented him with something he always enjoys—a challenge. Here was an opportunity to be a "first." Malcolm has been described as "the millionaire gentleman adventurer"—a somewhat hackneyed but nonetheless apt way of putting it.

Preparations for the trip began. Passports were updated. Applications for the various visas were made. Routes were planned. Departure was to be from Munich in West Germany on the morning of June 20. If the Russian visas were issued, we'd follow Itinerary Number One to Moscow. Our standby itinerary (Number Two) would take us to Berlin, Warsaw, Budapest, Bucharest, Sophia and, maybe, Istanbul.

For a while the potential membership of Malcolm's motorcycle gang fluctuated; eventually it settled down to an even half-dozen people (lately referred to as "The Siberian Six"). They were: Malcolm (Leader of the Pack), his daughter Moira (also known as Mighty Mo and the Forbes Heiress), his son Robert (usually called Bob, sometimes Bobby, occasionally Robert the Unflappable), journalist Lammy Johnstone (whom, for some inexplicable reason, I often called Tammy—much to her annoyance), photographer C. V. Augustus (hereinafter known as just plain Chuck) and myself (who got

Cruising the Communist countryside, the gang rumbles *from Wroclau to Warsaw.*

dubbed Our Macho Man by Mo and Lammy, but if you want that explained you'll have to ask them).

Except for Bob, who joined us in Munich, we all came together for the first time at Kennedy Airport in New York City on June 13 when we climbed aboard the Concorde and flew off to Paris. At this point, we had all the necessary visas—but the Russian ones. It appeared we would have to settle for Itinerary Number Two.

Another great enthusiasm of Malcolm's is ballooning and he was hosting a hot-air balloon rally on the grounds of his little place in Normandy—Chateau de Balleroy—that weekend. The four days I spent there could make a separate article (working title: "Citizen Forbes"), but I'll stick to our motorcycling adventures here. However, it was on Saturday evening that Malcolm announced to his dinner guests (several hundred of them) that, after some eight months of trying, he'd just received word that our Russian visas had been issued. Itinerary Number One after all . . . and just three days short of our planned departure from Munich. That's how close it came to not happening.

The visas were obtained via roundabout means. Malcolm had appealed to his friend Dr. Armand Hammer, who contacted his friend Russian Ambassador Dobrynin, who contacted his friends in Moscow. The Soviet government issued our visas as a favor to Dr. Hammer. Like they say—sometimes it's not what you know (although I found it amusing to speculate as to who may have known what about whom in this particular instance).

It was drizzling in Munich when our plane from Paris landed. We taxied to the Jahreszeiten Hotel, the best in Munich (which is what you quickly come to expect when you're traveling with Malcolm), where our jovial spirits of high expectancy were suddenly dashed. With little more than twenty-four hours remaining before we were to leave, the motorcycles weren't ready. The Hondas were still mostly accessory-less; the requested fairings and saddlebags had not been installed. The Harleys, which had been taken to Harley-Davidson's facilities in Frankfurt for preparation, were still on a truck somewhere between the two cities.

Malcolm was displeased. And Malcolm can be quite persuasive (all the more so when his mood is a bit truculent). Result: All five ma-

Bob Forbes poised with the bikes in Munich, the starting point. Destination: Moscow.

chines were in the underground garage of the Jahreszeiten by the next evening; complete with needed accessories and gassed up, ready to go.

On the highway northeast of Munich, some of the riding habits we were to use for the remainder of the trip began to evolve. Malcolm led the gang on his Harley Classic 80 followed by Bob on a Honda CBX or me on the Harley 74. Mo took turns riding behind the three of us. Lammy was next to last, still grumbling because the custom saddle she wanted for the CX500 had not been available. She could barely reach the ground; did a lot of ballet dancing herding her cycle at parking time. Chuck brought up the rear on the Honda Four, which was just as well, as it turned out. Before the day was over, he provided us with fodder for witty repartee when he became our first casualty by dropping his heavily loaded (all that camera gear) 750 at a gas stop. We didn't know then that he was only making a practice run for what was still to come.

Early in the afternoon we reached our first border crossing, the edge of Czechoslovakia. We'd heard some pessimistic estimates as to how long it would take to cross. We established a pool, betting on the time required. My guess of a half-hour, the shortest estimate, won me the first pot when we were ready in about twenty minutes. The guards raised the gate and together we all rode into the lands behind the Iron Curtain.

MSF's old case carried the spares.

On the Road to Moscow · 93

We reached Prague (which, according to the signs, now had become Praha) and its ancient narrow cobblestone streets in late afternoon. Our immediate priority was to locate our hotel. For the first of many times I witnessed the Forbes Finding Formula in operation. Malcolm would ride up to the curb and raise his helmet visor to converse with somebody standing on the sidewalk. He'd ask his questions in English; get his replies in the local language, nod nicely—and off we'd go. I didn't (still don't) understand exactly how this procedure worked—but it did. After only a couple of such multilingual conferences, he would lead us directly to whatever it was we were looking for. In the case of our hotel in Prague, he

Through the twisting streets of Prague, we left a wake of astonished pedestrians.

We'd heard pessimistic estimates as to how long it would take to cross into Czechoslovakia, but in 20 minutes we were behind the Iron Curtain.

led us right to it. But the Intourist folks had shifted our reservations to another of their hotels without bothering to let us know.

The bikes were hastily repacked and Malcolm put an alternate version of the Forbes Finding Formula into action. A taxi driver was

hired to lead us to the Olympic Hotel. He was in a bigger hurry than we were. We passed quickly through the twisting streets of Prague, leaving a wake of astonished pedestrians pointing out our strange procession to their friends.

After we registered, we discovered the hotel's telephone-booth-sized elevators were marvels of modern technology. They would lumber up and down more or less at random, stopping at floors where they weren't supposed to, refusing to stop where they were supposed to. As occupants, about all we could do was hope for eventual rescue. (They'd charge at least $2.50 for a ride like that at Disneyland.)

It had been a long day and after we showered and changed clothing, we were more than ready for food. We gathered in a big dining room only to be notified by a rather indignant waiter that all tables were reserved for large tour groups—which we weren't. He directed us to another dining room, where we ran headlong into a logistics problem. The tables there were set up for four people. There were six of us. No, we couldn't push two tables together. No, we couldn't move two more chairs to a table for four. No, we couldn't be served if there were less than four people at the table. Besides, they were closing shortly. Pushed to desperation by approaching malnutrition, Malcolm referred the matter to the hotel desk clerk who referred it to somebody else who summoned the manager who, upon learning of our predicament, herded us outside and down to a cafeteria-type lunchroom in the same building. We were shown to a large table already occupied by a gentleman who seemed not the least disturbed when six strange foreigners took over the remainder of his table. Things had become very communal all of a sudden.

He was an English-speaking Canadian; a convert to communism. That provoked the first of several fascinating philosophical discussions I was privileged to overhear in which Malcolm explained the advantages of capitalism. Neither man altered his politics, but they remained amicable in their differences. The food, when it finally arrived, was considerably less than gourmet grub. It was more twenty-four-hour greasy spoon than Chateau de Balleroy. And the wait-

ress certainly wasn't working for tips. Perhaps it was because Czechoslovakia was my first encounter with people under a communistic government but, in retrospect, it seems to me the Czechs were less cordial and more morose than the citizens of any other country we visited.

The next morning a local reporter claimed Malcolm for a breakfast interview. (He was nearly late; he had to take the elevator to get there.) I went out to pack my cycle and check the bikes for possible maintenance needs. I found a small group of curious people examining the machines. I was able to inform the group around the cycles as to the displacement of each machine. When one guy pointed at Chuck's Honda Four and, with his fist, indi-

Ubiquitous Communist Party symbols always tickled our capitalist fancies.

On the Road to Moscow · 95

As leader of the pack, Malcolm got to do the map reading.

cated a piston going up and down, then held up four fingers and raised his eyebrows, I nodded. He said "ah." Then I used his piston gesture, held up six fingers and pointed at Bob's CBX. There were gasps of amazement, and I lost my audience as it quickly regrouped around the big Honda.

Most of the morning was devoted to a taxi-led tour of Prague. We had picked a driver who seemed unaware he had five motorcycles rushing along behind him, running traffic signals,

hopscotching trolley tracks and ducking wet, mossy cobblestones in a desperate effort to stay unlost. It made for an exciting way (not) to see Prague. At one point a truck driver, who had the right of way, took considerable and very audible umbrage when all five cycles cut him off. His harangue caused me to be grateful that neither Mo nor Lammy understood the language—until I realized that neither did I and yet his meaning was most vivid to me.

Following an audience with the Ambassador, we engaged in another taxi-led flight through the streets of Prague; stopped only when we reached the highway leading to the Polish border. Malcolm had a variation on his taxi-led approach for any individual cartography puzzles. He made it a point for everybody to know the name of the hotel where we had reservations at our next destination. The theory was: Should anybody become separated from the group, he could always hire a taxi driver of his very own and thus return to the fold. The first flaw in the scheme came when none of us knew the name

The Czech countryside and small villages were devoid of any advertising—except that extolling the Party.

Hopscotching trolley tracks is tricky, especially when there are live trolleys on them.

of the hotel where we were supposed to stay that evening in Wroclaw (used to be Breslau). Somehow Malcolm had misplaced the reservation voucher. Well, we'd face that problem when we came to it, he decided. (Malcolm doesn't believe in worrying.)

Leaving Czechoslovakia was a simple process. Not so checking into Poland. What with the delays in filling out currency questionnaires, custom declarations, exchanging money and the time required to do this, that and all the other others, it required more than an hour and a half before the inevitable gate went up and we all rolled off on Polish roads. (Bob won the pot that day.)

By late afternoon we were on the outskirts of Wroclaw. Alongside the road was a sign bearing the official Intourist insignia, a lot of Polish words and an arrow indicating a side road we were rapidly approaching. Malcolm made a quick decision. We turned onto the road, followed the arrow and soon pulled up in front of a motel-looking hotel which had Pepsi-Cola umbrellas around the swimming pool.

"I've thought it over," Malcolm announced as he dismounted. "I'll go to the desk pretending this is the hotel where we have reservations. When they don't have them, I'll get upset. Probably they will get on the phone and call the other Intourist hotels to find out where our reservations really are. That will save us the trouble of having to do it for ourselves." (Malcolm really knows how to delegate.)

"Well, if that doesn't work," I suggested, "you can always buy the place." (Fortunately, Malcolm's sense of humor includes the ability to laugh at jokes made about Malcolm Forbes.)

Leathers squeaking, he strolled through the entrance; reappeared very shortly, looking both disappointed and somewhat surprised. "I didn't get to use my speech," he complained. "I went

to the desk and as soon as I told the clerk my name, she smiled and said, 'Yes, Mr. Forbes. We've been expecting you and your party.' This is our hotel."

Of all the Intourist hotels in Wroclaw, we had by chance picked the correct one.

The next morning we continued to Warsaw. Beyond Wroclaw the highway passed through a few villages, roamed across green rolling hills and among ripening fields. I was leaning back enjoying the vista when Lammy pulled up alongside me and motioned at the Honda's tank. She was on reserve. A gas station was located in a little village and when we arrived, I led the herd of cycles into the service area, much to the dismay and evident annoyance of the attendant. He had several reasons for being upset. First, we'd come in from the wrong direction, completely ignoring the no entry sign. Second, a tanker truck was replenishing the gasoline storage tanks and the station wasn't open for business at the moment. Third, when it did open, there was already a string of vehicles lined up (and on the proper side) for servicing. And finally, we didn't have the necessary fuel coupons, so he couldn't sell us gasoline to begin with. Other than that, everything was copacetic.

Tourists need fuel coupons if they're using their own vehicles. These coupons can be purchased at banks, hotels and other places transients are inclined to patronize. Malcolm and Lammy located a nearby hotel and set off to find some coupons. The rest of us lolled on our

Our day's rest in Warsaw happened to coincide with a full military parade, right in front of our hotel.

parked cycles and entertained the growing crowd with our mere presence. Bob unpacked his sound/movie camera and took shots of the group with Mo at the microphone doing the narration. Later on I learned that when Mo took over the mike at such times, she was doing her impersonation of Gilda Radner impersonating Barbara Walters. I became used to suddenly hearing Mo say in a lisping voice—"This is Baba Wawa weporting" — from wherever we happened to be at the moment. Baba turned up in some pretty strange places. Once I encountered her during rush hour in the Moscow Metro (subway), where she remained totally unflustered when I impulsively asked her for directions to Times Square. The Forbes progeny are adaptable, and they have a lot of fun doing it.

About the time the truck finished filling the storage tanks, Malcolm returned with a fistful of coupons. We were permitted to crash the line; even allowed to do so from the wrong direction. Evidently, the attendant wished to rid his establishment of this public nuisance we'd inadvertently become. By then the curious crowd was beginning to overflow into the street.

As the day's road captain, I managed to lead us through the maze of traffic and general confusion of the city of Lodz in an efficient and magnificent (I thought) manner. I felt it went a long way to make up for the wild chase I'd led them on in Wroclaw. Beyond Lodz, however, the weather—which had been consistently per-

fect since we'd left the chill and drizzle of Munich behind—turned cloudy and then damp. At the next gas stop we got into rain gear and Malcolm took over the lead again. The rain wasn't heavy, but it was persistent. We turned our headlights on (a procedure we began to use all the time in order to make it easier for the leader to check on his flock). Not too many kilometers down the road from the gas stop I realized there were no motorcycle headlights reflecting in my rear-view mirrors. Malcolm made the same observation. We pulled over and waited—and waited. The rain-shrouded road behind us contained no evidence of motorcycle occupancy.

Obviously "something" had happened. Dreading what we might find, we turned around and started back. A few kilometers down the highway, a single headlight blurred through the mist. Bob and Mo on the CBX. Then two more cycle headlights. Everybody apparently was all right, but Chuck's 750 looked a little bit different than it had the last time I'd seen it (about a quarter of an hour earlier). The left roll bar was laid back against the engine case it had saved. The windshield was missing a big chunk of plastic. The handlebars might have been twisted just a tweak. Chuck had indulged in an altercation with an automobile while he was passing another vehicle; went for a slide down the wet asphalt. It almost was a head-on-er, but Chuck remained undaunted, if slightly bruised, and the Honda remained rideable.

It was clearing when we rode across the bridge into the beautiful city of Warsaw. Malcolm immediately resorted to his people-on-the-street interviews and shortly we were in front of the Hotel Intercontinental Victoria (which would be our last taste of fancy living for a while).

We were scheduled for a one-day layover in Warsaw. That gave me a chance the next day to check over the cycles, which were at rest in

the hotel garage. Both Harleys were down on oil. While I was wondering where one went in Warsaw to purchase Harley oil, Lammy and Chuck appeared in order to examine the damage done to the 750. I explained my problem. Lammy has a knack for finding out just about everything about anybody. She quickly determined that the two garage attendants were not

Trim, grim, and keeping in step.

above a little blackmarket dickering for the Castrol 20W50 in their possession. Dickering became bickering when it came time to hand over the cash. They refused our Polish money; wanted Western currency, which they favored over coin of the realm—preferably Deutsche marks or American dollars.

Eventually, we and the garage attendants came to a mutual agreement, a process which involved an hour or so of cash-counting, outstretched

A peaceful counterpoint to the military parade was found in Wilanowek, a Warsaw suburb where this former royal palace still stands. The gardens give *the many visitors a chance to pause and reflect on a slower, earlier time.*

An old Polish hero, Prince Poniatowski, still charges into battle, while centuries later schoolchildren enjoy a day off. (BELOW) The Lazienkowski Palace's ballroom has floors that are polished and ready for the music to start.

palms, shaking heads, muttered oaths in sundry tongues, much turning and walking away for several steps before spinning around and returning at the top of one's voice, and many other procedures common to monetary bargaining. But we had our oil—at a cost of approximately $2.50 per quart. I replenished the cycles and the excess was stored away in saddlebags for future reference.

The following morning we set out for the next lap of our trip. Our ride that day was to be a short one; only about 200 kilometers (roughly, 120 miles). But it was a day long on expectations. The date was June 24 and we would cross the Russian border.

We moved the cycles to the front of the hotel to simplify the loading process. When I was almost ready to go, I realized I hadn't seen Bob since he'd parked his CBX some time earlier. The machine still wasn't loaded. I asked Mo if she knew where her brother was.

"Uh-huh," she answered. "He's in the elevator."

"Elevator? What's he doing there?"

"Trying to get back his bungie cord."

While bringing his luggage down from his room, Bob had managed to get a bungie cord caught in the elevator door. Evidently it then worked its way into the operating mechanism. Bob, his luggage, and several other passengers had managed to get out, but Bob was minus the cord—and the hotel was minus one operating elevator. Repairmen had been summoned. We had some extra bungies but—the next time you're in Warsaw, please check the Hotel Intercontinental Victoria and let me know if the center elevator is working. It wasn't when we left town.

We were checked out of Poland much faster than we'd been checked in. It was al-

most as if our exodus had been expedited (perhaps a report from the hotel?). Beyond the Polish border station we passed through a short section of demilitarized area which halted abruptly at the Russian border (where the soldiers all carried submachine guns).

Then, there we were—six people, five motorcycles—on the edge of Russian territory. We rode up to the lowered gate where Russian soldiers stood on either side of the road, looking at us with expressionless faces. One soldier stepped into a small sentry house. Through its windows I could see him talking on a telephone. We waited, engines idling. Beyond the gates the road continued for a short distance, then curved to the left to disappear among trees. No structures were visible.

The soldier stepped out of the sentry house and said a few words in Russian. Another soldier moved up to operate the gate. It went up slowly. Russia straight ahead. With Mo on behind him, Malcolm shifted down and the Harley moved across the line. First American cyclist

A tense moment: the Russian border. We were let in one by one, not seeing or knowing what had happened to the one of our party who'd gone just before we were beckoned.

into the Soviet Union. I kicked my machine into low and let out the clutch. As I began to move forward, the gate came crashing down in front of me. I hit the brakes. There was a lot of shouting and yelling. The soldiers were motioning me back. I stared at them in astonishment. They frowned back at me, pointing and muttering. They made it obvious that I wasn't going anywhere at that particular moment. I sat there watching as Malcolm and Mo grew small and then disappeared around that bend in the road.

I turned around to exchange puzzled looks with the others. Immediately behind me Robert the Unflappable merely shrugged his shoulders. We sat some more. The soldiers seemed to have forgotten we were still there. I put the Harley on the kickstand and turned off the engine. It was quiet. Very quiet. You could have heard a firing squad from miles away, I thought.

The moments went by slowly. My anxiety built. Then there were some more Russian words. The gate swung open once more. This time the soldiers made it very clear that only I was to proceed; the others were to remain where they were. I started the cycle and, with a halfhearted and fully forced smile, and with what I hoped appeared to be a friendly wave at my uniformed friends, I rode across the line. The gate came down behind me. I've never felt so alone as I did at that moment. It was an eerie experience which each of us underwent in turn. We were admitted to the Soviet Union one by one—by ourselves. Apparently it was routine procedure to permit only one vehicle to enter at a time—and with a time interval between each. But when that vehicle is a motorcycle and the rider crosses the border in all his exposed solitude, it tends to promote attacks of paranoia.

As I rounded the bend I could see a large

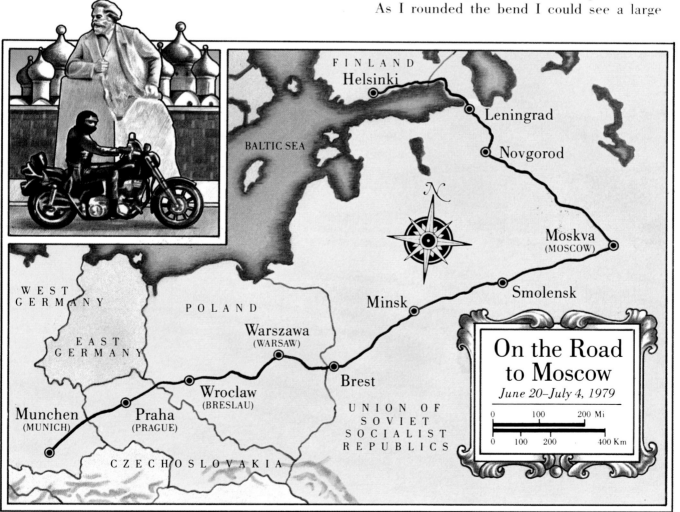

On the Road to Moscow
June 20–July 4, 1979

building ahead. Mo, Malcolm and the Classic 80 were the center of a small group where most of the men wore uniforms. I rode up, acutely aware of all those eyes focused on me. A stern-looking soldier approached and held out his hand, indicating he wanted my passport and visa. I gave them to him. He flipped the passport open, examined my photo there and looked back at me; another glance at the photo and a closer look at me. Then he barked an order of some kind. I didn't have the slightest idea of what he'd said. I turned to Malcolm and asked: "What am I expected to do now? Kiss his ring?"

"He merely requests you remove your sunglasses, please. Presently he is uncertain as to your identity," I was told in precise but softly accented English by a stocky, richly mustached man dressed in civilian clothing. That was my introduction to Anatoly Pascoe. (It also taught me never to assume that nobody within hearing distance of us understood English.)

A man in his early thirties, Anatoly was our official Intourist guide; would accompany us throughout our stay in Russia. He was a past Soviet boxing champion, a weightlifter of some renown, and, in general, a superb physical specimen (which he subtly demonstrated on several occasions). That qualified him to serve as our bodyguard as well although that point was never verified. Nor were our suspicions that he might also be a representative of the KGB (roughly analogous to our CIA).

Anatoly did not ride motorcycles. He traveled in an automobile driven by a solemn man named Vladimir who, to my knowledge, did not possess a last name. They planned to lead us across Russia, but we convinced them to follow us instead, thus permitting us to set our own pace. At first we greatly resented Anatoly. We felt his presence a threat to our freedom of adventure. The limitations imposed by his constant observation would, we thought, change us from venturing nomads to prisoners in transit.

On the other hand, his interpreting ability was a big help from the start. After aiding us in the filling out of all the forms and declarations, he conveyed to us a request from several of the soldiers—they would appreciate our permission to photograph our motorcycles. They

could; we couldn't. Photos of border stations (among many other things) were not permitted. We had Anatoly tell them to help themselves. They posed for each other's cameras on our cycles and wearing our helmets and, in the process, ceased to be the formidable guards we thought they were. Instead they were a bunch of youths having a great time. Probably they'll never know how much that episode helped get us off on the right foot in our attitude toward the Russian people.

Whereas Anatoly was taciturn, Michael Bruk was gregarious. Mike, who worked for Occidental Petroleum in their Moscow offices, was Dr. Armand Hammer's representative, sent to help ease our way. He had flown to Brest, our first Russian destination, to meet us and even though he had been waiting all day, he was cheerful and full of explanations—some for questions we'd not yet asked.

Once the border-crossing formalities were out of the way (a process requiring an hour or so), Mike and Anatoly climbed in the automobile and with Vladimir driving, led us into Brest. As we pulled up to the hotel, a wedding was being celebrated. A large group on the sidewalk was cheering on a middle-aged lady who was somewhat unsoberly executing a folk dance. With our arrival, she decided to select herself a partner: Malcolm. (Was she coached or was it just a woman's intuition?) He paused only to remove his helmet before he responded in kind. In his black leather pants and biking

It's not too hard to figure out which way to Moscow. Though the language was tough, with signs like these we figured we could get to the capital city.

A capitalist blessing for the happy couple.

gear, he did his best (which was pretty damned good) to follow her movements. The crowd—including all of us—loved it. My border-crossing paranoia receded some more. Obviously, the natives were friendly.

But we had to hurry. Please check in and prepare for the tour as soon as possible. Tour? What tour? The official tour. We were to be shown the Brest war memorial. Such evening tours became routine. At each destination along our route, cars would appear with English-speaking guides who were experts on the local points of interest. They escorted us to explain the tourist attractions—most of which had me wishing I'd brushed up on my Russian history. At first we tended to regard these tours as a chore; a duty to be performed in return for the Russian hospitality. Soon it became something to look forward to instead of merely endured. It's one thing to see an ancient landmark or structure but quite another to know what you're seeing and to be able to have your questions about it answered immediately.

It was late when we returned to the hotel. As I examined the lights of Brest from my hotel room window, I found myself looking forward to tomorrow. We'd been accepted; the Russian people were beautiful. Not even Chuck's questioning the placement of our rooms—one above another instead of all on the same floor—bothered me. "Are rooms easier to bug that way?" he'd asked. I didn't know. I didn't care. I relaxed and enjoyed a pleasant sleep.

The cycles spent the night locked in a garage which was tended by a small, elderly lady who wore an enormous cheerful grin across her wrinkles, and a faded babushka over her gray hair; she was almost too quaint to be believed. We claimed the bikes early the next morning. Then we discovered a couple of things about Russian restaurants and breakfast. First, they don't open until eight o'clock. That's the start of the working day so don't expect to grab a quick bite and get on the road with the rising sun.

While waiting for the restaurant to open, I was out checking the cycles. Suddenly I heard "This is Baba Wawa weporting to you diwectly from Bwest, Wussia—where I'm slowly dying of hunger. . . ." Bob and Mo were killing time.

Finally, we were ready to go. Vladimir took the wheel; Mike and Anatoly made themselves comfortable in the back seat. We followed them to the highway, then the car allowed us to pass and take the lead. The terrain was similar to

The ladies on the truck. This was how the robust road crew got to work each morning.

the American Midwest; rolling plains with lots of wheat fields, a few low hills, occasionally forests. But for the most part we rode all day down a straight, tree-lined road. It wasn't the most exciting ride in the world.

The helicopter which kept passing back and forth overhead helped to pep things up. So did the frequent police guard houses we were passing; two-storied affairs looking somewhat like stunted airport control towers. Often there was a police motorcycle/sidecar rig nearby at the ready. The police would scrutinize us as we passed. Behind us, our "guides" kept pace. All this combined to cause a return of the paranoia.

There weren't many places along the road where food was available. Lunchtime was long gone before we finally spotted a sign for the

At filling stations, our KGB guides managed things so we could bypass any vehicles waiting in line. Gasoline lines? Yes, though not from a fuel shortage; it's a shortage of stations.

next cafe. This time the structure we found at the specified distance down the road was a filling station, not a lunch room. We continued for a short distance and decided we must have missed it. As we stopped to double back, the car horn began honking and Vladimir motioned for us to continue ahead. In the confusion Bob took the lead. A couple of kilometers more and we could see a village with some modern structures off to the right of the highway. Maybe the cafe was located there. A police tower stood at the crossroad leading to the village—as they do at most rural intersections. As Bob turned toward the village—immediate panic. Police were shouting and blowing whistles. Bob stopped halfway around the curve. The rest of us were ordered—by use of police batons (a polite way to describe them)—to pull over. One officer, evidently in charge, spouted a lot of rapid words which made it plain he knew we were supposed to be going to Moscow. The road to the village was not the way to Moscow! We must continue on the highway. Were we under some sort of surveillance? Or was it just that the only three Hondas and two Harleys within about one thousand miles were kind of hard to miss?

Apparently Mike and Anatoly had been napping. Now they were wide awake. Mike chatted with the officers; learned the cafe was located in the trees behind the filling station. We went back for lunch but by then I'd lost my appetite for anything much except some of the great Russian black bread.

Vladimir always watched our cycles when we were away from them. Habitually he remained mute; apparently did not speak English (at least not in our presence). But he was in his glory as our official motorcycle sentry and took enormous pride in explaining our machinery to his curious countrymen. I don't know what he told them, but invariably they were impressed. Association with those cycles enabled Vladimir to climb a rung or two on his social ladder.

Mike had a talent for shooing people about with a few curt phrases. He was a genius at clearing the way for us. As we approached Minsk, the highway widened into four lanes again. Near the edge of the city a policeman in front of one of those towers obviously was preparing to stop us. Suddenly the guide car flashed past us. In the front seat Mike was leaning across Vladimir, shouting apparently most declarative sentences at the startled cop. (Russians rarely converse; mostly they shout at one another.) Properly chastised, the cop let us continue unmolested. It puzzled me. Why had he accepted Mike's word? Later, when I had the opportunity, I examined the car to see if I could detect any sort of official emblem or other marking which might distinguish it. Unless it was contained in the license plate, there was nothing. But the same thing happened again later as we were entering Moscow. I concluded it wasn't the car; it was Mike.

That night in Minsk, Mike announced he was flying back to Moscow, where he would meet us in a couple of days. Now we had to rely on Anatoly, who had remained more or less in the background while Mike was present. Anatoly had not yet gained our confidence. Where Mike directed, Anatoly endured. Mike inspired immediate trust. With Anatoly it took a little longer—but it also lasted longer, as we learned in Moscow.

En route to Smolensk the country became more hilly and the ride more interesting. There were frequent gaps in the trees lining the road, permitting us to catch glimpses of forested hills, pastures and meadows. In the fields farmers were at work—sometimes with contemporary farming machinery; sometimes with

Lenin, Father of the Revolution. This alabaster bust is available in a state-owned, foreigners-only gift store.

two-handled scythes and wooden rakes. A country of contrasts.

"What are we doing here?" I asked after we had followed Malcolm into a small parking area that contained a couple of well-used trucks. To one side stood several dilapidated structures, long overdue another coat of their green paint.

"Supposed to be a lunch stop," Lammy told me.

"This is Baba Wawa weporting to you diwect from . . . where are we?"

I watched Bob and Mo shoot some film, then we set out to find the others who had disappeared. One building was a cafe—more or less. Malcolm and Chuck had settled down at a small table enjoying a glass of something which turned out to be made from birch sap. It was good; the food was not.

Often, Bob would ride ahead to find places where he could photograph the rest of us as we passed. Chuck decided he would do the same thing, so he left the lunchroom early and was gone when we returned to the parking area. Mo was riding behind me that day and about 20 kilometers on down the road, she leaned forward to ask if we'd passed Chuck yet. We hadn't.

More kilometers. Still no Chuck. We were about half an hour from the lunch stop. Mo tapped my shoulder. "I'm worried about Chuck," she said. "Suppose something's happened to him? He couldn't have gone the wrong way, could he?"

"Having shared rooms with him since Munich," I replied, "I wouldn't be at all surprised."

We rode on and on—and then, suddenly, a 750 Honda flashed past us at what must have been full throttle. Chuck, of course. Sure enough, he'd turned the wrong way as he left the lunchroom. He had found a place to stop and had waited with his cameras ready for about twenty minutes before he realized his mistake. Well, I thought, at least they ain't picking us off one by one.

Vladimir blew it going into Smolensk. We ended up on the wrong side of the tracks (if they have such places in Russia). Malcolm, who had been quietly educating himself in the art of reading Russian road and street signs, took over the guide duties and without a single man-on-the-street interview, maneuvered us into the center of the city.

After two days in Russia I had learned there is no place to obtain a drink of water during the day's ride. I was parched and as soon as we reached our hotel I changed and went to find a beer or something. Malcolm had beat me to an unadorned room which contained a cafeteria-style counter, plus several tables and chairs. That was the bar. He was seated at head of the largest table, surrounded by a group of young Russian students, one of whom spoke halting English. Our lady Intourist guide also was present to help with the interpreting. The students insisted on buying—and what they bought was a sweetish, bubbling wine (strawberry derived,

A brief summer shower brought out umbrellas (which were not considered decadent luxuries).

I believe) for which I developed an immediate fondness. We all sipped and conversed—mostly about politics. Evidently the name Malcolm Forbes was not unknown to the students. This time the capitalism versus communism comparisons took us into the fields of music (they knew Gershwin, Porter, Berlin, Ives, Copland, et al., but named Russian composers I'd never heard of) and sports (great anticipation for the 1980 Olympics) as well as military generals. If they knew about Grant and Lee and Pershing and Bradley, how come we couldn't name many famous Russian generals? They made their point. Russians are considerably better informed about Americans than Ameri-

Also available at the gift store are copies of the great "Worker and Collective Farm Girl." The original graces the entrance to the Economic Achievements Exhibition in Moscow.

cans are about Russians. Our debate ended in a friendly draw.

Moscow is some 375 kilometers from Smolensk (about 235 miles). The next morning was June 27, the day Forbes' Foragers would invade the capital of Russia. Even NBC television was going to be present to cover the big event (Lammy had made use of her journalistic connections). Because they were not permitted to venture more than 40 kilometers from Moscow without special permission, the television crew

arranged to meet us approximately that distance out of the city. We departed early, just to be sure we'd be there at four o'clock, the time NBC had specified.

Crossroads became more frequent and villages more numerous. The highway widened into four lanes again and, at major intersections, became a maze of converging lanes and multiple signal lights. As we approached one such series, they began to blink green. I'd already learned that blinking green was equivalent to amber. It meant, stop. (Amber, on the other hand, appears at the end of the red cycle and is the signal to go again.) Malcolm was already in the intersection; I was too close to stop in time. We both proceeded through and Malcolm continued right through the second blinking signal. I stopped. A policeman summoned Malcolm. He pulled over. When the light turned amber, I started up; got motioned over as well. The others joined us at the side of the highway while the policeman, discovering we didn't speak Russian, copied down the license plate numbers of both Harleys.

"What's going to happen?" I asked Anatoly when he arrived. "Do we pay a fine or get tossed in jail or what?"

"Ah," said Anatoly, "that we shall find out later." (And I thought the Chinese were supposed to be the inscrutable ones.)

Discovering we didn't speak Russian, the policeman copied down the plate numbers of the miscreant Harleys.

The sky had gradually darkened. It began to sprinkle rain. The sign read: Moskva—43 km. We proceeded slowly through the rain and found what passed for a rest stop about 35 kilometers from Moscow. We stopped in the large parking revetment next to the highway where, back among the trees, was a lean-to with a bench. Lining up the cycles so the people from NBC couldn't miss them, we retired to the lean-to. We were almost an hour early. It was raining harder. We huddled under cover and ate chocolates from a large box Mo had produced from Malcolm's tour-pak; washed them down with bottled water from my saddlebags. We were now more than one thousand kilometers into Russia, and we were ready for Moskva.

But was Moscow ready for us?

II

AN AUTOMOBILE turned into the parking area; stopped alongside a large truck (one of the few tractor-trailer rigs we saw in Russia). The truck driver exited his cab into the rain; exchanged parcels of some sort with the occupants of the car. The auto departed in one direction; the truck in the other. I wondered what sort of transaction had taken place. Russian air tends to hone one's suspicions.

As the thunderstorm moved on, the rain lessened. A car turned into the rest stop, hesitated, then circled the parked motorcycles. On the passenger side, a head with a camera for a face took picture after picture of the bikes. Our curiosity about their curiosity grew as we watched. Then somebody recognized the driver of the car—Michael Bruk. When Mike had left us in Minsk, he'd said he would see us again in Moscow. I hadn't expected him to go to all the trouble to drive out and meet us.

When the rain had faded to a light sprinkle, Yuri (who spoke English a little) requested we pose with the motorcycles. Immediately, Malcolm went to his magic tour-pak. Earlier that morning he had brought out the fishing gear so

When the darkened sky unloaded the rains 35 km from the Kremlin, we pulled into a rest stop. We were ready for Moskva. But was Moscow ready for us?

mysteriously purchased in Smolensk. With duct tape he had attached a section of the pole to the back of the saddle of the Classic 80 where it would serve as a makeshift flag staff. Now he produced his flag—a dark-blue scarf inscribed with red letters in a pattern which repeated over and over the *Forbes* magazine slogan, "Capitalist Tool." In the absence of an American flag (which we unsuccessfully attempted to obtain along the way, only to find that not even the American Embassy could supply us with

one), the scarf was to serve as our standard. It continued to flutter from the fishing pole on the Harley for the remainder of our trip.

The posing session was over; Mike was ready to leave. "Come on," he urged. "Let's go into Moscow."

We explained about NBC.

Mike didn't hesitate. "Didn't I tell you? I'm sorry. NBC called my office. They can't make it, but they will see you in Moscow."

Evidently some big news story was breaking; something more important than the arrival of the Forbes Expeditionary Force. Well, win some; lose some. We climbed onto the bikes, ready to set about to invade Moscow, determined to succeed where Napoleon and Hitler had failed.

Anatoly and Vladimir rode in their car behind us but were hanging farther back than they usually did. As had happened before, Anatoly tended to recede into the background when Mike was present. Yuri was hanging out the

window of Mike's car, shooting dozens of photos of us as we rode along posing so we wouldn't look as if we were posing. Mike drove alongside us, then ahead of us, then behind. Yuri didn't miss an angle.

For photographic purposes we were holding a tighter riding formation than we normally did; nevertheless, my mind was preoccupied with a dark thought. Why had NBC called Mike? Lammy was the one who had contacted the network's Moscow offices. I wasn't aware that Mike knew about the arrangements. More importantly, I wasn't aware that NBC knew about

After the rain, busloads of Pioneer Youth (a sort of Communist Boy Scout organization) poured into the rest stop. Soon capitalist MSF was besieged for autographs.

Mike. When we reached the hotel, Lammy's curiosity bit hard. She called her friends at NBC. They weren't in, she was told. They were out on the highway west of Moscow waiting for a bunch of American motorcyclists.

"Mike sabotaged our television coverage," Lammy told me. "Why?"

Once Yuri had enough photos, he settled back into the car. Mike took the lead and the pace picked up considerably. We began passing buildings. The highway widened into a boulevard. Mike maneuvered us to a center lane which was reserved for emergency vehicles and VIPs in transit.

With Mo riding passenger, Malcolm led the cycle contingent. Bob and I alternated second position, both of us shooting photos from the saddle. Then my camera ran out of film and I began to concentrate more on what I was passing. The Minsk highway became Kutuzov Pros-

pekt, a wide thoroughfare lined with stately, often elegant buildings. The profusion of political billboards increased; some covering the entire side of buildings several stories high. The hammer and sickle, Lenin and others, usually in red, were all over the place. So were big red stars.

We sped by Victory Square with its Triumphal Arch topped by a large statue of a chariot drawn by six horses. Directly ahead was a tall, double-winged building intended to resemble a

This is what you get when the tank-design collective updates a '56 Chevy.

Russia, full of contrasts.

Yuri half-emerged from the car window again, his camera pointed back at us. We turned one way for a few blocks, then another. Quickly we passed a part of the Kremlin, October Revolution Square, the Metropol Hotel (being renovated) and the Bolshoi Theater. A few more turns and we were stopping in front of the Intourist Hotel on Gorky Street, just a short walk from the Kremlin and Red Square.

The crowd began to gather before we could back the cycles up to the curb. We turned off the bikes, looked at one another smugly, and dismounted. We had made it. Moscow. I asked Mo what she thought of the city so far.

huge opened book. We crossed the low, wide bridge across the Moscow River at its base and veered to the right onto Kalinin Prospekt, which would lead us into the center of the city. We passed rows of tall contemporary buildings; older, more ornate structures, as we rode past them on remarkably clean streets. At least three distinct schools of architecture were evident. Moscow was a striking city but, like all of

The Great Patriotic War, WW II to us, is a theme featured throughout Russia. The contributions of the Allies diminish under Russian memories of 20 million dead.

The road into Moscow became the Kutuzov Prospekt, a wide thoroughfare lined with stately, often elegant buildings. In spite of the excitement, Moira managed to nap along the way on the back of MSF's bike.

She sheepishly replied that she hadn't seen it yet.

"After all that jogging around we just did? The quick guided tour? How could you miss it?"

"I was asleep," she admitted. Ever the sophisticate, Mo had chosen to doze as she made her big entry into Moscow behind the unsuspecting Malcolm, who had thought all their helmet bumping had been the result of a lot of looking around.

"Very unprofessional," I kidded her. "It wouldn't happen to Baba Wawa."

Malcolm collected our passports, routinely needed when checking into a hotel, and with Mike went into the lobby to complete the room arrangements. I loaded my camera with fresh film and backed into Gorky Street. Early on I'd learned that any time I was about to take photos of a crowd, it was best to fiddle with the exposure and focus for a moment. That gave anybody who didn't want to be photographed a chance to back out of camera range. Almost always somebody did.

We would be here for a couple of days. I unpacked everything I thought I might need and left the rest in the bike luggage. Gathering up all my gear in my arms, I began to edge through the crowd toward the hotel entrance. A youngish man appeared alongside me. "You come from America?" he asked. His English was coated with a thick accent, but he spoke deliberately and slowly enough to be easily understood. I told him I did. "You go back to America?" I said such were my plans. "I would talk to you about America."

"Fine. Okay. Be happy to."

He took hold of my shoulder. "We talk now?" I said I wanted to get all my stuff inside first. He pulled me back a step. "I would like to give you a gift," he said softly, "from the peoples of my country to show friendship. I would give you a Soviet phlig." He was offering me a rolled-up newspaper which obviously concealed something.

"Well, thank you. I appreciate that. But— my hands are full—if you'll just let me get this stuff into . . ."

"I fix," he said. He did. The newspaper-wrapped phlig was poked under my arm, above all those plastic bags of clothing I had clamped

to my side with my elbow. The whole mess began to slip. I pressed harder; walked faster. The doorman/guard opened the doors for me and I entered the hotel lobby. He didn't. I saw him watching me through the big windows of the lobby, hanging back from the entrance. Puzzled by his refusal to enter the hotel, I headed toward the registration desk.

What the hell is a "phlig," I wondered—and how soon does it go off? A newspaper headline flashed across my imagination: "Mysterious American Terrorist Blows Up Moscow Hotel Lobby. Device Used Said to Be Phlig."

I was almost to the desk when my gear ava-

Ranking with France's Eiffel Tower and Egypt's Sphinx, St. Basil's Cathedral in Red Square evokes Russia. This time it was covered in scaffolding for an Olympic renovation. (BELOW) We never failed to draw a crowd, as motorbikes in Russia are functional and not used much for pleasure. Such high-cc touring machines had never been on Russian roads before.

Much Lenin, little Stalin

lanched onto the floor and ended up in a big pile next to Chuck's luggage (he had detachable saddlebags). The rolled-up newspaper had stayed under my arm. I removed it. It was soft. I didn't hear any ticking. Gingerly I began to unroll the newspaper. A bit of red fabric appeared. More red material with gold on it. This was a phlig? I unrolled more. It was a flag. A Soviet flag. Quickly I rerolled it, fearful somebody might have seen. But why did I feel guilty about being in possession of a Soviet flag? And why had the Russian given it to me so furtively?

He was waiting for me outside. "Very nice," I told him. "Thank you again. Very much."

"Now, we talk of America?"

I explained there were reporters waiting; that our schedule would be hectic for the rest of the evening and suggested we postpone until the next day.

Tourists, mostly Russian, tour the towers and museums of the Kremlin.

Great Patriotic War statuary abounds.

The profusion of political billboards increased, with some covering entire sides of buildings several stories high.

"It is not possible," he sighed. He had to "go back where I come from" early in the morning. I suggested he meet me in the lobby later. That was not possible, either. As a Russian he could not enter the hotel (which was strictly for tourists) without a pass. That explained why he'd waited outside. We settled on meeting outside the hotel about 10 P.M.—and I warned him I might be late.

I was; it was nearly 11 P.M. when I walked outside the hotel. There were few people on the street at that hour. None of them was my friend. I smoked a cigarette and waited; finally decided he'd given up on me or something. It was the "something" that bothered me the most. Was he merely interested in America (as so many Russians are)? Or was he looking for information which might help him defect to the

The year was 1979, so the forthcoming Moscow Olympics were being promoted heavily.

On the Road to Moscow · 119

Western world? And there was a third possibility, too. Could he have been a KGB agent testing us to see how we might respond should we be approached by a potential defector? I never did find out. I never saw him again.

We had two full days in which to see Moscow. The guided tours began the next morning when Mo, as Baba Wawa, had a chance to "wepowat to you diwectly from Wed Squawe." Anatoly joined us during the days, aided the first morning by another Intourist guide, a pleasant lady named Valentina. As we stood in Red Square watching the line of people waiting to visit Lenin's tomb, I turned to her. "I may be asking the wrong question," I prefaced my inquiry, "but I know that at one time Stalin's body also was in that tomb. But it was removed. Do you know where Stalin's body is now?"

"Oh, yes. His grave is immediately behind

We were told that even in the dead of winter there's a line waiting to see Lenin in his tomb. This fine summer day the Lenin line was 6 hours long.

Lenin's tomb . . . and why do you say you ask the wrong question?"

"Well, I understood that Stalin isn't mentioned much in the Soviet Union these days."

"Oh, no. That is not true. Stalin is one of our great heroes. However, he is not as great a hero as Lenin, so it was judged inappropriate for his body to be in Lenin's tomb." After she told me that, I kept an eye out for signs of Stalin. On several occasions I saw photos of him and once I saw him featured in old newsreels as a part of a television documentary.

Fortunately, our tour that morning was done in automobiles. The rain returned and often we would remain in the vehicle and gaze at the sight we were seeing through rain-freckled win-

The Moscow Metro is an awesome contrast to what New Yorkers know of subways. Each station seemed more decorated than the last: mosaics, statues, busts, chandeliers, stained glass. And the claim that trains run on time was verified by a huge digital timer that started on departure of each train. By the time it reached 90 seconds a new train would be there.

In case you forgot who was boss . . .

dows. In the afternoon our mode of transportation altered and we took the subway. Anatoly did the guide duties. We were accepting him as he strived to be helpful and please us, all in his own unobtrusive way. Eventually we made him laugh and, eventually, made him an honorary member of the Forbes Expeditionary Force.

Anatoly led the safari into the maze of the Metro; down a fancy escalator into an even fancier subway station. Each seemed more decorated than the last; mosaics, statues, busts, chandeliers, stained glass—beautiful things which would last about two seconds in a New York subway station.

The claim that trains run every minute and a half was verified by large digital clocks which started counting the seconds as a train departed. The next one always arrived before the counters reached ninety seconds. The cars had a certain air about them—as did most of the public places we visited, including the GUM department store. It was the smell of people.

"These folks never heard of Right Guard," Lammy complained.

Between stations we surfaced for a session in

Minsk, like Moscow, is a "Hero City" for its losses and courage during the war.

an art gallery where Malcolm put his discerning eye to work; made several purchases to be shipped back to the United States. Then we hurried back to the hotel for a late afternoon press reception arranged by Mike and hosted by Malcolm. Lammy had asked Mike if the American media representatives in Moscow had been invited. He assured her such was the case. Her curiosity prompted her to make several phone calls and she discovered that such was not the case. She invited them. Mike didn't seem to mind when some of them showed up, but Mike Bruk's stock dropped two or three more points on our exchange.

When Malcolm first expressed interest in cycling to Moscow, I suspected that one of his reasons might have to do with a display in the Kremlin. He is justifiably proud of his Fabergé art collection, said to be second only to the collection in Moscow. On our second morning in Moscow, we set out for the Kremlin and the Fabergé.

I'd always thought of the Kremlin as a specific building. It's not. The word means "fortress" and almost every Russian city had its Kremlin; an ancient, walled city that became the hub of an expanding community. Within Moscow's Kremlin there were many palaces, cathedrals, residences, office buildings and meeting halls. Anatoly guided us through the grounds to the Armory, which housed a fascinating collection of historic objects and works of art. Many were once possessions of various tsars (a word that came from Latin and was abbreviated from "caesar")—Ivan the Terrible, Peter the Great, Boris Godunov, the Romanoffs, Catherine the Great. We saw thrones, carriages, armor, sleds, ceremonial costumes, crowns—most of which contained gold and gems.

Then, finally, the Fabergé display; a collection of miniature objects intricately wrought from rare metals and precisely decorated with jewels. The famous Fabergé Easter eggs, routinely commissioned by Russian royalty as gifts, hold a special attraction for collectors. We tarried to marvel at the Fabergé display for as long as possible; backing up other tour groups behind us. I suspect there may have been a bit of

envy involved when Bob announced his tally of Fabergé eggs.

"I'm afraid they've got us by one egg, Dad."

After lunch we were to fulfill a request from the press to pose with the cycles at Red Square. We'd not used them since we'd arrived and when we went to retrieve them, they had been moved. There was a muddy footprint on the saddle of the Harley. As I brushed it off, the lid of the tour-pak rattled. It was loose. I was sure I had locked it. I had, but the lock had been knocked out. The saddlebags had undergone the same treatment. I'd been robbed (which struck me as a rather capitalistic practice). Nearly everything I'd left in the bike was gone —cold-weather gear, heavy gloves, Damarts, sweater, my prized and irreplaceable favorite rain suit, souvenirs from the Concorde flight, oil, chain lube, chewing gum, extra cigarettes, even half-used books of paper matches. They had left me one bottle of water and—inexplicably—the tool kit for both Harleys.

Malcolm's machine had been hit, too. But only one saddlebag; the other one and his magic tour-pak remained locked, their contents intact. The fact caused us to wonder if we'd interrupted the thieves at work. Lammy's CX500 had a trip trunk permanently attached to the luggage rack. She hadn't bothered to lock it because all she left in it were several cans of oil. They were gone. The Hondas all had de-

The lid was loose. I was sure I had locked it. I had, but the lock had been knocked out. I'd been robbed, which struck me as a rather capitalistic practice.

On the Road to Moscow · 123

tachable saddlebags which had been taken to the rooms, so there were no other losses.

Photographers were waiting. Malcolm set the damaged saddlebag lid to one side and we rode over to pose at the base of the Spassky Tower. Anatoly went over behind Malcolm; returned with me, more to satisfy his growing curiosity about our obsessions than anything else. He seemed to enjoy the experience but was not convinced he should take up motorcycling.

"It is considered quite dangerous," he told me as we waited for a traffic light to change. "There are places in my country where motorcyclists are omitted from the census rolls. It is felt to include them would be a wasted effort." I never did decide if he was kidding me or not.

We returned the cycles to the basement, where Malcolm discovered that the saddlebag lid he'd left behind had joined the list of missing items during our absence. There wasn't time to conduct a search. Limousines were waiting. We had an appointment with the mayor of Moscow. (Technically, his position was closer to that of chairman of the city council.)

We were ushered into his palatial offices and seated along one side of a long conference table. Mayor Promyslov, his aides and Mike (who had come along to do the interpreting) were seated on the opposite side. While we partook of his tea and cakes, Promyslov told us about Moscow. He talked of future plans for the city, preparations for the Olympics, expansion of the Metro— and he spent considerable time explaining why there was no crime in Moscow.

Not one of us had the guts to tell His Honor we'd just been ripped off in his fair city.

Mayor Promyslov presented Malcolm with the key to the city. The Mayor was amused when MSF returned the favor by giving him a "Capitalist Tool" necktie and a scarf for his wife.

Malcolm and Promyslov discussed a variety of subjects, occasionally augmented by comments or questions from the rest of us. The meeting ended when Mayor Promyslov presented Malcolm with the key to the city of Moscow. (Later we found identical duplicates on sale at the souvenir shop for just a couple of bucks.) Malcolm returned the favor by giving the mayor one of his "Capitalist Tool" neckties and a scarf like our flag for his wife. The mayor seemed amused.

That evening the task of filing a report on the robbery fell to me. I had lost the most stuff and knew more about the cycles. I collected any information I thought might be needed—engine numbers, missing items, approximate value—and went to an office off the lobby to meet with Russian law enforcement officers. It was a little

Prominently displayed in his office were progress photos and a large electrified map of how the city would handle the next year's Olympics. Hosting the games was about the greatest thing to hit Russia since they invented the tractor. The U.S. no-show was quite a blow.

more than half an hour before I was to join the others for dinner. That, I guessed, would be more than enough time.

I was shown to a desk, handed a ballpoint pen (a surprise; ballpoints and chewing gum are regarded highly in Russia) and a paper tablet. One officer spoke to a lady from the registration desk who was to interpret. She turned to me. "First," she said, "it is required that you put down the date." I did. She had me read it back. She translated.

The Russian officer interrupted her. "Nyet! Nyet. Nyet, nyet, nyet, nyet." He added some other words. She turned back to me.

"It also is required that you put down the name of the day."

That's how it went; line by line. I wrote. I read it back to her. She translated to the officer. He'd break out in an attack of "Nyets," then tell her what he wanted next. She'd tell me, each time prefacing her instruction with "It also is required that you add . . ." (The English phrases heard most frequently in Russia are: It is required, it is not permitted, it is impossible, and, it is misunderstanding.)

The time to meet the others for dinner passed. I mentioned that fact several times; was told it would require only a minute more. Finally it was required that I add my signature.

I signed the pages and stood up, assuming we were finished.

"Nyet! Nyet. Nyet, nyet, nyet." I was waved back to the desk as the officer conversed rapidly with the lady interpreter.

"It also is required . . ." she began.

My turn to interrupt. I had lost my temper. "Right now," I declared angrily, "it is also required that I get my butt up to the dining room and tell my friends to go ahead without me. I'll be back in a few minutes." I stalked out, turning to catch a quick glimpse of their startled faces as I exited. One does not—definitely does not—walk out on Russian police officers. The situation was so unthinkable that apparently they didn't know how to handle it.

The others were waiting at a table; not for me but for service. Without Anatoly or Mike around, it had become a problem. I asked them to order for me when they got the chance and returned to conclude the police business.

We finished rather quickly after that, then adjourned to the basement to examine the damaged saddlebags. (The attendant who had thrown Bob out of the garage wasn't around; in his stead was a man I recognized as one of those who had witnessed the episode.) From what I could make of the conversation between the attendant and the officers—this based on the lady's response to my questions—this guy and the other dudes who worked at the parking garage had been greatly puzzled by the unusual behavior of the American motorcyclists who had refused to park their machines in the garage where they would have been guarded. Their theory was: We must have been misinformed by our Intourist guide. He was trying to hang the blame on Anatoly.

When we returned to the lobby, the officer had the woman thank me for my cooperation and suggested they might want to examine the cycles again later. I told him he'd better make it quick because we were leaving for Novgorod in the morning. He didn't like that answer; steps might have to be taken.

"Sounds to me as if they're gonna make Anatoly the goat," I reported to Malcolm, "and, even worse, they hinted they might try to impound the cycles as evidence."

Malcolm, as usual, had a solution: Mike and

Wreaths at the tomb of the unknown soldier; Malcolm and daughter Moira with our guide and by-now friend Anatoly.

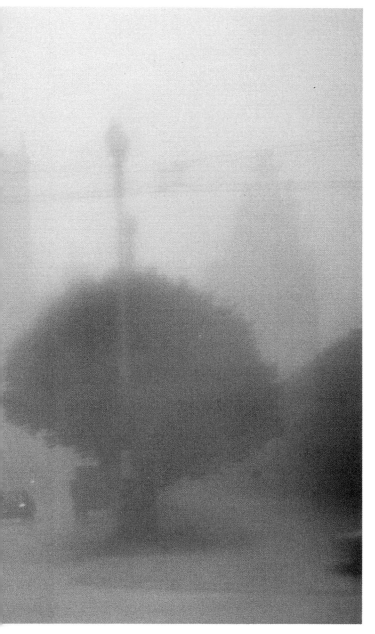

Moscow U. peers through another summer shower. All grads are guaranteed a job. And they'd better take the one assigned.

his marvelous talent for shooing people around. And Mike was on hand early the next morning when we went to pack up the cycles. Also on hand was Malcolm's missing saddlebag lid; it had been returned during the night.

Anatoly arrived. I grabbed him, explained what had happened and how they might try to blame him. Anatoly seemed resigned. "Let me tell you a story," he sighed. "A few years ago there was a railroad accident. Many people were hurt. There was an investigation to determine who was responsible. It was determined that the railroad tracks were not at fault, therefore the maintenance crew was blameless. The engineer was determined not to be responsible. The conductor was not at fault. Eventually it was determined that the person responsible was the ticket taker—because he had allowed all those people to get on the train."

I didn't know if Mike's shoo-ability was responsible or not, but there was no problem in reclaiming our cycles. Mike cheerfully bid us farewell. It was good to get back on the road, this time from Moscow to Leningrad. The weather was great and we were passing through many more villages than we did coming from Brest to Moscow. People always stopped to watch us go by.

The country was hilly. We were seeing more forests, more lakes and more rivers. We

On the Road to Moscow · 127

Malcolm enjoys his after-lunch cigar.

pressed on at a pretty fair clip. This was our longest day; more than 500 kilometers. The perpetual problem of finding lunch while on the road came up again. When we finally pulled into a lunchroom which had been indicated by one of those knife and fork markers, it was closed. Malcolm was anxious to reach Novgorod. We outnumbered our chairman so we

voted ourselves a break. Malcolm loves the process of riding but constantly keeps each day's destination as his immediate goal. There's not much procrastinating for sightseeing when Malcolm leads the pack; not much time for routine maintenance, either. I doubt if he would ever tighten a chain without being reminded. He's anxious to get started and, once underway, he's anxious to arrive.

Twice we'd passed a big truck (it had overtaken us while we were stopped for gas) and both times the Russian driver had leaned out the cab window hollering and cheering us on. Evidently he'd seen the article in the sports newspaper; it had appeared that morning. As we lingered over our cigarettes enjoying the rare break, here came our good trucker buddy around the curve. He pulled his rig to an immediate stop and ran back to us. He didn't speak English, but he had concluded we were hungry. He wanted to tell us about his favorite trucker's cafe which was only about 20 kilometers up the road. Through Anatoly we got the details and decided to give it a try.

It wasn't marked with the "approved" knife and fork sign, a fact that seemed to cause Anatoly some concern. It was back off the highway, a large asphalt parking area with an Alpine-

In a throwback to former times, this food store is a showcase for edibles produced in the Soviet Union.

looking building facing on a small lake. When we entered, there were people waiting for seats at the large communal tables, but we were made welcome and shown to a small balcony and a table all our own. The specialty (and almost total menu) was potatoes and sausage, fried together and served in the pan. The beverage was called "Questa" and was made from black bread, soaked in sugar water and allowed to ferment. Traditionally it is served two mugfuls at a time on the assumption that refills will be requested. The meal was—to my famished appetite—most tasty; my favorite on-the-road meal of the entire trip.

Clouds had been accumulating all day; the rain began as we arrived in Novgorod. (We unpacked the cycles quickly and took them to the hotel's basement, where the garage attendant enthusiastically welcomed us and examined our machines knowledgeably. I half expected him to tell us about the Harley or the Indian he had owned when he was younger. Obviously, our bikes were in good hands for the night.)

Leningrad was only a couple of riding hours away so we took our tour of Novgorod the next morning. The city, which celebrated its one thousandth anniversary in 1862, is the most an-

Domes and spires of the Cathedral of the Smolny Convent, described to us as a former girls' school; it now houses the Museum of the History of Leningrad.

The entrance to the new Hermitage Museum adjacent to the Hermitage, which was formerly the Winter Palace.

cient of all Russian cities. We had time to absorb only a tiny fraction of its history, to see only a few of its sights. The most famous, St. Sophia's cathedral, is now a museum (as are most cathedrals in Russia; for the nearly eight million inhabitants of Moscow, there are only forty-one places of worship remaining —this for all faiths).

As New York is to Moscow, San Francisco is to Leningrad,

On the Road to Moscow · 129

a city whose beauty belies its bloody history. Built on a series of islands, it boasted many bridges and, as once the capital, many palaces. Our hotel, the Astoria, almost qualified. It was built around the turn of the century and retains much of the elegance it must have had back when royalty was still around. The lobby was the grandest we'd seen since Munich. After I had taken my luggage to the room, I returned there to find Malcolm.

"I think I've got the wrong room," I told him.

He grinned. "You didn't expect that, did you?" What I hadn't expected was a large two-room suite furnished with antiques, a huge bathroom with heat, a large television set, a refrigerator, heavy velvet draperies, and walls covered with a textured fabric. Suddenly there was luxury in Russia. I had no doubt many names from history had passed through the Astoria. Hitler wasn't one of them. He had planned to celebrate the conquest of Leningrad (formerly Petrograd or Saint Petersburg) at the Astoria, even sent out invitations. It never happened. Russians kept the German troops from entering Leningrad.

We had the next day to tour Leningrad, aided

Survivor of the battle of Tsushima Strait in 1905, the cruiser Aurora *is now a revered icon of the Revolution. In accordance with Lenin's plan, from her decks was fired the shot that signaled the storming of the Winter Palace.*

On the night of October 25, 1917, the Winter Palace—residence of the Tsars and seat of the last government of the bourgeoisie—was taken by storm by Red Guardsmen and Revolutionary units of the Army and Navy.

Through the arch of the General Staff building and into the Palace Square poured the revolutionaries.

by an Intourist guide named Sonja, who seemed to enjoy our company and was particularly fond of discussing politics with Malcolm as she pointed out such things as the Winter Palace (also known as The Hermitage and closed the day we were there), the Art Museum, Lenin's headquarters during the revolution, the Naval Museum and the cruiser *Aurora* (which Bob had been looking forward to since the trip began).

Tuesday, July 3, 1979. Our last day in Russia. Anatoly had startled us in the course of our "last night" dinner the evening before when he had announced he would not be accompanying us to the Finnish border. It tended to put a damper on the dinner, which was particularly extravagant at the Astoria. Our initial resentment of Anatoly had altered to one of respect, friendship and, we were suddenly aware, dependence.

On the Road to Moscow · 131

"Do not worry," he advised us. "You will have no trouble without me. It will be easy. Tourists do not have problems when leaving the Soviet Union."

The car led us to the highway toward Vyborg and Leningrad. At the outskirts of Leningrad, it pulled over to let us pass. We all waved our final farewells; even Vladimir acknowledged our gestured thanks and good lucks. Then, for the first time in Russia, we were totally on our own.

Anatoly had been right. There were no big problems; just several little ones. At several police towers, we were stopped. The officers always checked out our cycles (sometimes asking questions about them), but it was apparent they were also checking us out of Russia, station by station. It was both disconcerting and, somehow, strangely reassuring.

Beyond Vyborg we hit the worst road we traveled in Russia. A new highway was being built, and the old one simply ceased to exist at times. Enormous ruts, deep sand, huge, fist-sized rocks. At points it was barely passable. And we stacked up three crashes within minutes. Lammy did a pas de cheval in the sand; took her usual bow. Chuck's handlebars turned floppy again, and so did he. With Mo on behind him, Bob encountered a car in what should have been a one-way section of sand, pulled into deeper sand to avoid it; spoiled the CBX's until-then perfect score. That left Malcolm and me bragging about being the only ones who remained vertical during the entire trip.

We checked out of Russia, rode several miles across a buffer area before we arrived at the Finnish border where the guards stared at us awestricken. One came out of his trance long enough to raise the barrier and let us in. Another who spoke English apologized. "I have been at this border crossing for many years and never have I seen one motorcycle come out of the Soviet Union. Suddenly, we see five of them!"

Border procedures went quickly and we rode off into Finland and the Western world—and the sun came out! The beautiful day bloomed brighter. The change was something felt, not seen; not one big thing, but hundreds of little ones. Mostly it was the reappearance of things we had forgotten; not missed until they returned. Bright colors, precise highway striping, service stations with restrooms, bottled-drink machines, cups of coffee, signs advertising products, familiar names such as Shell or Coke, a Kawasaki 400 parked on the street, more cars than trucks on the road. Even the landscape seemed to brighten.

(Malcolm led us into Helsinki as the rain started and soon resorted to his street interviews in order to locate our hotel. It wasn't necessary. While he was conversing with a pedestrian, Bob started pointing. The hotel was directly ahead, less than a block away. More luxury.) As we dined we made plans for the next day. We would take a look at Helsinki, attend an afternoon reception at the American Embassy in celebration of the Fourth of July, put the cycles (and ourselves) on the ferry for the overnight crossing of the Baltic to West Germany. I went to bed thinking I could sleep in.

At eight o'clock Mo knocked on my door. "Want to go back to the United States?"

"Oh, eventually. I'm kinda enjoying this. Why? What's up?"

Malcolm had been talking to New York. (He made frequent and, no doubt, expensive cross-Atlantic telephone calls throughout the trip.) His New York offices would like him to return as soon as possible. Lammy's publisher requested her immediate presence. Malcolm had arranged for seats on a noon flight.

The panic began. We were rushing this way and that all over Helsinki; purchasing luggage to replace what had been stolen in Moscow; finding a place to leave the cycles for crating and shipment; dozens of small errands. The folks at Otto Brandt's Honda came to our rescue; got us to the airport in time.

By one in the afternoon we were taking off from Helsinki. That evening we were in New York, where the farewells were quick and so casual it was obvious we had not yet realized it was all over. It was a day with many extra hours, but later that night I was landing at Tulsa (where my cycle had been stabled in my absence) and watching the last of the fireworks exploding in the summer sky.

The Great Adventure had ended, not with a winding down, but with a bang.

It was the perfect way to celebrate the Fourth of July.

When we had completed our tour of Leningrad, Sonja asked to see the motorcycles. I walked with her to the area where they were parked, listening to her tell of other Americans she had guided through Leningrad.

"Happy Rockefeller was here. We went into a store. She saw something there she liked but when she learned it cost about ten of your American dollars, she decided not to buy it. She said it was too expensive. She is very rich. I do not understand Happy Rockefeller.

"American Judge Burger and his wife came to Leningrad. Mrs. Burger complained that she was here at the wrong time. At her home it was the season for canning. She said she should be there preserving vegetables. She said when she returned the price of vegetables would be higher. She, too, I do not understand.

"But, Mr. Forbes. Ah. Mr. Forbes is a rich man. But he knows how to enjoy his wealth. He enjoys spending his money. He enjoys his life. He spends his money to make himself happy and to make his friends happy. Now, Mr. Forbes, I can understand."

I'll drink to that (preferably Chateau La Tour Haut Brion, if you please).

MSF with Bob and Moira in Red Square, paved heart of the Communist world.

On the Road to Moscow · 133

6
CHAPTER

In the Land
of the
Midnight Run

Allan Girdler

SHORTLY AFTER 3 P.M. on what the French call 6 juin we left Omaha Beach and pointed the bikes inland. It was the thirty-sixth anniversary of D-Day, first step in the liberation of Europe, and it was a good time to ride a Harley-Davidson across France.

It was also something of a diversion.

Malcolm Forbes likes to ride motorcycles and he likes to ride them to different places, places most people only see on maps. He's ridden all across the U.S. and Europe and he tends to do everything he does as completely as it can be done. (After he got interested in balloons he sank a cool million in a round-the-world balloon. Alas, he crashed on the launching pad and narrowly escaped, a history which becomes germane later in this account.)

Forbes is a student of history, naval warfare included, and he knew that the northernmost part of Europe is known as the North Cape. Hundreds of miles north of the Arctic Circle, the cape figured large in World War II as the

Cruising along the steppes, above the timberline between the Arctic Circle and North Cape.

place you had to get around. The cape is the farthest north, the closest to the North Pole, that you can go on wheels so Forbes decided he'd like to ride there.

For most of us, impossible. For Forbes, a matter of detail. He enlisted me, his son Bob, nephew Duncan and a friend of the younger Forbes, Dr. Jan Enezelius, a Norwegian physician who was saddled with the job of planning the routes and stops. I got to take notes, Bob and Duncan are professional photographers. Distinguished company, I thought.

For Forbes, getting five bikes some five thousand miles across territory none of us had seen was logistics. The Harley Electra Glide he rode across Russia in 1979—first time that's been done, by the way—was in England, so he had it shipped to his chateau in France. He'd just bought an FLT, so that was delivered to the chateau. He already had one Honda GL1000 there, so Bob rode the English GL to and off the boat, and Duncan brought his brand new Yamaha XS850.

The scenery is incredible: like Glacier National Park for 1,000 miles. From fjord to tundra, through green fields and mountain meadows with sparkling blue lakes—and all with snowcapped mountains in the background for good measure.

That made five motorcycles for five riders and it didn't even make a dent in the Forbes stable. People who have money and enjoy it don't live like the rest of us.

Idea was, we'd ride across France, Germany, Belgium and a corner of Holland, then take a boat to Norway, at the top of which is North Cape. So as to spare you the details of my summer vacation, I'll leave out the ride across the known parts of that section of the world.

Mostly, it's like the U.S. If you pick the scenic route you go through small town after small town, getting lost and getting stuck behind big trucks and small cars towing camping trailers.

If you pick the autoroute, autobahn or motorway, you're on roads like our interstates. Except that in the U.S., the morally superior pig the fast lane at 55, while in Europe the morally

In the Land of the Midnight Run · 137

smug drive fast cars and terrorize the fast lane at 100 and up.

I got the first hint of this trip's secret pleasure when we crossed from (I think) France into Belgium. It was raining and we sloshed into the booth where you swap francs for marks. The man in charge knew we were Americans and he took me into his office. There on the desk, pride of place in his decal collection, was a sticker. He was a member of the Harley club in Holland. Didn't own one, never figured he'd have the money, but Harleys are his passion, so on the way out, me being on the FLT at the time, I gave him the full rumble of the big Twin.

Actual highlights here were putting people's noses out of joint.

We tend to think that only in America are motorcycles frowned on. Not so. Europe has been able to afford cars for a generation, so they reckon bikers are crazy, just like at home, and when we walked into the various four-star hotels and restaurants—Forbes lives well—we got chilly stares.

But in this case, we were riding with a man who lunches with presidents and has kings as houseguests, and the hotel manager rushed out to be sure the bikes were secure, that we approved of the rooms. We lunched in leathers while the chef wrung his hands, because Forbes has been known to make public his disappointment in gourmet places.

The other patrons—may they slobber pâté on their neckties—didn't know what to think. Just goes to prove the truth in the adage Living Well Is the Best Revenge.

We took a ferryboat from Germany to Norway and, to my way of thinking, we escaped from Europe.

Norway is wonderful. Until this trip I hadn't really thought much about the country. I mean, it's part of Scandinavia, they build ships, and that's all.

First, the place is huge. Well, not so much big as long and thin, about 1,200 miles long and 280 miles wide. Norway is the northwest coast of Europe. Mountains, lakes, pine forests and such.

The roads are good but not too good. No autobahns, no arrogant Mercedes drivers. You'll get a lovely smooth four lanes, then two, then oiled dirt with a construction detour or perhaps a tunnel with no lights and a dirt surface pocked by holes, terrifying. Not dull. Lots of curves. What you do in Norway is ride, rather than just sit there.

Next, the taxes are awful. On the order of 100 percent, meaning that if a Kawasaki 1300 sells for $5,000 equipped, the taxes add another $5,000 and yes, we met some guys with $10,000 Kawasakis and Suzukis. Good to remember when we bitch about U.S. prices.

The good side of that, for Americans anyway, is that because they take your money in the showroom, they don't have to take it in court. They have advisory speed limits and we saw a

The roads are good, not dull. Lots of curves. What you do in Norway is ride rather than just sit there.

total of two patrol cars in a couple of thousand miles. If you drink and/or crash, they lock you in so deep Christmas carols arrive in June, but failing that the police are not a revenue agency. You can ride as fast as conditions permit, in short, and that's fast.

The scenery is incredible. Like Glacier National Park for 1,000 miles. Green fields, sparkling blue lakes, snow-capped peaks. The first few days we didn't ride more than an hour at a time as the photographers had to shoot everything in sight. After that even they got used to colors the developers won't believe and we just hummed along, saying to ourselves Gee, another sparkling lake with snow-capped peak.

Travel tips: All the guidebooks I've seen talk about border crossings and papers, etc., but although I can't say you don't need all the papers, we didn't have any trouble at borders. We went through the borders of France-Belgium, Belgium-Holland, Holland-Germany, Germany-Norway, Norway-Finland, Finland-Sweden and Sweden-Norway with nothing more than a brief glance at passports. If that. Couple of the borders were closed for rain and holidays, if you can believe that.

Next tip is for Harley-Davidson. Once upon a time the American motorcycle was the standard of the world. We made the biggest and strongest and we sold them overseas, even taught the Japanese how to make them. Things changed and it will not come as a surprise to hear that nowadays the U.S. is well on the losing side of the balance sheet.

But, Harleys have fans everywhere. Soon as we were spotted by bikers, they had to see the Harleys, talk about Harley, ask about cubic centimeters and prices.

Just as Forbes's international reputation got us into the Best Places, so did the Harleys make us heroes on the road. In one town, Alta, Norway, we asked directions to the hotel. The guy was on a KZ1000. Soon as he told us where to go he zoomed off and got his pals, the three guys in Alta who had Harleys.

They came thundering up the driveway on their Sportsters with drag bars, shotgun pipes, extended front ends, just like home.

We were having a spot of trouble, as it hap-

Land of the
Midnight Run
June 6–June 23, 1980

pened. A truck pulled in front of Forbes on a detour and he dropped the FLT, something one does not do lightly. He was bruised and needed a rest; the T's fairing was askew. The 74 had broken a wire on the rough dirt road and the battery was flat, which I didn't know until it wouldn't crank over.

The lead Harley man looked at the T and commented that it was leaking oil. Yes, I said, blushing in shame, we haven't had time to fix it. Forbes was fascinated by the exchange. First that this guy had spotted instantly something Forbes wouldn't have seen in a year, second that I had writhed with the loss of status that comes from arriving on this dream machine that wasn't in tiptop shape.

But one of the bikers invited us to his shop, where he charged the battery, helped with the new wires and the whole crew volunteered to aid in getting the T back in alignment. If the hotel was full, they offered, we could stay in their clubhouse. As it happened we pushed on to another posh resort, but the offer was appreciated.

As a gesture of thanks we bought the first round and let the Norwegians sit on the FLT. Yeah, I know about taxes and import bothers and all that. But. If Harley ever decides to do

Malcolm and son at the crossing point. Note scrub grass and snow and general bleak aspect. The mapmakers' red line which traditionally marks the Artic Circle was nowhere visible.

something about the balance of payments and get serious about exporting, they have a potential market consisting of every bike nut we met in Europe. Meanwhile, it made me proud to be on a 74.

Along in here somewhere we crossed the Arctic Circle. Most satisfying. Not being a world traveler I wasn't sure what to expect, save that all the pictures I'd seen involved fur-lined parkas and sled dogs.

We rode up a pass through a mountain range and the trees got smaller and more scrubby, then disappeared. Raw grass, rocks, glaciers to the left and right, windswept granite and right at the top of the bleakness, with railroad tracks protected by covers as the snow can't be plowed from the tracks, was a sign proclaiming the Arctic Circle. The air was cold, the sun was

(BELOW) The Lapps are the Navajo of Scandinavia, in that they were there first, camp out, and sell services by the side of the road. (LEFT, RIGHT) Everywhere you turn, another postcard is waiting to be snapped.

A young reindeer watched us with considerably less interest than we him. (RIGHT) The first time I'd seen a "Caution—Moose Crossing" sign.

weak and by Admiral Byrd it surely did look like it should. I was glad I had two sets of woolies, then a wool shirt and sweater, then leathers under my thermal rain suit.

I was even more glad when we rode down the other side of the pass and found pine forests, then little farms and fishing villages. The Gulf Stream warms the coast of Norway so it's much warmer for its northern position than you'd think.

We took advantage of this by riding along the coast, with skips from mainland to islands and back on a series of coastal freighters and ferries. One freighter hadn't hauled motorcycles before and nearly dropped the FLT, but our shouts averted this and after that we were allowed to sling the bikes ourselves.

One of the reasons for the ride, aside from having an excuse to go riding I mean, was to see the Midnight Sun.

Fascinating. We had the route and stops planned so we'd get to go to the top of the world in time for the sun to not set. Longest day of the year in an area where they have no sunset for ten weeks.

When I first heard about this I spent some time with a globe and a lamp, figuring: If the sun doesn't set, where does it go?

Now I know. The sun moves in a big circle, as if a lasso artist was making a loop above your head.

When you wake up at 6 A.M. the sun is in the east, at about the place it would be at 8 A.M. in

the U.S. At noon the sun is due south, but it's risen to maybe 9 A.M. position. At 6 P.M. it's in the west, as it should be except that it's only dropped the equivalent of one hour. And at midnight it's in the north, hanging above the horizon and still strong enough to warm your face.

Strange. More strange was the loss of time sense and orientation. We'd get up at what seemed like midmorning, ride for eleven or twelve hours, have dinner, work on the bikes and go to bed at what felt like midafternoon, more tired than we felt entitled to be because obviously the day was still young. The natives adapt, they told us, but I never did.

Suspense. This freighter hadn't handled bikes before and nearly dropped one.

The trip wasn't properly a comparison test,

but twelve hours in the saddle every day for weeks do give some definition of what works on the road. Duncan's XS850 was by far the quickest. He would cruise through winding sections that had the Harleys dragging their floorboards. But the bucket seat did make for cramps and the tiny fairing wasn't enough wind protection for hours of running 80 mph. The Hondas were unperturbable, as always. Just loafed along, the Vetter fairings keeping wind and weather at bay. Halfway through the ride we thought we ought to check the Wings. One needed some oil, the other didn't, and that's the only service they got or needed.

Both Harleys needed to be checked over

We skipped from mainland to islands and back on a series of coastal freighters and ferries. Here Malcolm cools out.

every day and as it happened what maintenance we could provide minus tools and parts and supplies wasn't enough. Best part here was that you could tell who was on the Hondas because at 3 P.M. they were shifting from cheek to cheek, sitting on the passenger section, sitting on the tank, etc., anything for relief. But the Harleys, especially the Electra Glide with frying pan seat suspended on a hydraulic post, were comfy as easy chairs all day long. Fast cruising on secondary roads is what Harleys are made to do, and no machine does it better.

Finally. Cape Nord. There's a little town at the ferry stop, packed with tourists as you'd guess, then you ride 20 or so miles, up into the coastal mountains and right to the edge of the world.

Not a friendly place. Windswept, cold, no trees, land's end for Europe is a barren cliff with cold gray seas stretching as far as the eye can see. Just what I had hoped for, in sum. There's a cafe and a telephone booth and I nipped into the booth and called my wife, mostly to hear her voice but also to say we'd

made it and that the trip home would be all downhill.

And so it proved to be, except that there's more than one meaning to downhill.

With goal achieved, we picked up the pace. Back into town, back onto the ferry, back through what has got to be the worst tunnel in the world—made even more horrible on the return trip by the presence of a gravel spreader, yes, midway through. We'd thought the slime on the road was accidental but no, they haul it there on purpose. Two miles' worth, hitting potholes in the dark while trying to keep between invisible walls.

We emerged upright and headed for Finland, southbound and down.

As nighttime shortened, there was not much time for the moon.

We'd been running hard, 70 and 80, and slowed for a small-town pedestrian crossing when bang! *Malcolm's tire blew. Bad luck, good timing.*

We lost another bike when the clutch gave out, but we'd made our primary target: the North Cape. From here you can ride only south.

For a couple of days I'd been worried about the 74's back tire. The rough roads had taken a toll. Oh relax, Forbes said.

We'd been running hard, 70 and 80, with Forbes on the 74 for several hours. We slowed for a small town with pedestrian crossing and Bang! Soon as I heard it, I knew what it was and sure enough, the tire had popped and put Forbes across both lanes, lock to lock.

He'd been doing maybe 24 mph and kept the bike upright.

When we had our hearts going again, we reflected briefly on how it happened that the tire went just exactly at the only time all day it could have gone without serious consequences. Remember how the record-attempt balloon failed on the ground rather than at its planned 40,000 feet? Forbes overshot the land once on a coast-to-coast flight and set that balloon down nearly on the decks of some fishing boats that happened to be in the area.

Malcolm Forbes is a lucky man.

Not even the Forbes luck could interfere with the next event. We'd arrived at the height of the midyear summer holiday. I can't say that everybody in the Finnish town was drunk. Instead, everybody we met was drunk, all the stores were closed, there was no way we'd get a new Harley tire in less than a week, if then.

So we repacked and Forbes and son doubled up until we'd crossed the border into Sweden, closed, or maybe I should say open and unguarded, because of the holiday. Next morning

we took Forbes to the airport and the rest of us headed down the coast of Sweden.

Somewhere close to halfway, the FLT's clutch gave out. We towed it to a gas station, where we learned how seriously the Swedes take holidays. Everything was closed, there was no hope of parts or even a rental truck for two days. So that Harley, too, was parked to await rescue by the Stockholm dealer.

We were now four riders for three bikes, with gear lashed precariously everywhere. Tell you what, I volunteered, I've been where I wanted to go, how about you drop me at the railroad station?

Soon as they rode off around the corner, I discovered that in Sweden holidays are total. The first hotel I hiked to had closed the restaurant. The holiday. It was 8 P.M. and I hadn't eaten since before noon. I walked to a pizza place (closed) and a Chinese restaurant (closed) and a disco, open except touring leathers didn't meet the dress code. The other hotel was open but they, too, had succumbed to disco madness. No suit, no dinner. My explanation cut no ice with them, so I trudged back to the station and sat on a bench, wondering if, when the milk train arrived at 1 A.M., I'd have strength enough to climb aboard.

In walked a lady carrying a bottle of apple juice. Where did you get that? I blurted in English. From a restaurant that just closed, she said, adding that obviously my need was greater than hers, would I like the bottle?

Yes. Face to face with the first sympathetic person I'd met in Sweden, I told all.

How awful, she said, adding that she used to ride a BMW, she thought leathers were much more attractive than John Travolta Whites and finally, she was on her way home from a wedding, with leftovers, would I like them?

Yes. Cold meat, cold potatoes, dry bread and apple juice, wolfed down while sitting in the train station, four hours until the milk train arrives, was fine.

So I dozed my way south, caught the next flight to London and arrived at Forbes's English HQ, a manor with even a ghost.

Forbes got home just about the same time, having gone for some business meetings in Germany, and he was sorry to hear the other Harley had failed.

But he wasn't discouraged. The FLT could be hauled back to the Stockholm dealership and put right, then shipped to France or England or wherever he figured he might want to ride a Harley.

The Electra Glide, though, had already been across Russia and now Scandinavia, and it was

Europe's north edge is marked by this striking sculpture a few feet back from the cliff. From left, Robert Forbes, Dr. Jan Engzelius, MSF, nephew Duncan Forbes, and the author.

bound to be a little tired. Forbes had been reading the motorcycle newspapers and he'd learned that there was a brand new Wide Glide in England. He has one in New York and likes it, so the thing to do that morning was go visit the dealership and work out trading the old bike for a new one. Would I like to come along?

Sure, I said.

Being rich is fun.

The midnight sun. At about 12:15 A.M. June 18, 1980, at Hammerfest, Norway, the sun was still above the mountains, strong enough to warm your face and to ride without lights.

7

CHAPTER

CHINA

Tim Forbes

MALCOLM FORBES was determined to inflate his balloon next to the Great Wall of China. In black leather boots and black leather pants, he stepped over the steep brown mountain slope, among scrawny evergreens and tangled brush, an invading Mongol general contemplating his next advance. But nowhere could he find shelter from the winds sweeping down from the steppes to the north and up from Peking to the south. Finally, in the last slanting rays of afternoon sun, he gave the order to unfurl the 74-foot hot-air balloon in the cramped parking lot between the Great Wall and the small souvenir shop. The wind punched a belly in the balloon just where the Chinese and American flags crossed, turning it into a spinnaker. Malcolm

and his team persisted. The wind shifted, blowing the balloon back against the electrical wires that fringed the parking lot. They did not give up. And then, at last, abruptly, nature seemed to surrender. As the balloon rose 5, 10, 20 feet, tugging at its tethers, a crowd of foreign tourists and Chinese workers let out a cheer. For the first time ever a hot-air balloon was floating above the only man-made structure on earth that, a new myth has it, is visible from the moon. It was a historic moment, a sight to remember, a triumph of persistence.

The Chinese philosopher Lao-tzu said that even the longest journey begins with a first step, but this journey began with the last step of another journey. In 1980 Malcolm Forbes led the first American motorcycle team into the Soviet

Union. Upon completion of that expedition, it occurred to Malcolm that the People's Republic of China remained the last major country on earth in which no Americans—in fact no foreigners—had yet motorcycled and ballooned. The temptation sounded too good to resist. "Firstness," explains Malcolm, "is always fun. And it's the one record that no one else can break."

The trick was to get invited. Malcolm approached former President Richard Nixon, who wrote a personal appeal to Chinese Deputy Chairman Deng Xiaoping. Nothing happened. Malcolm asked former Secretary of State Henry Kissinger to see what he could do. Those efforts got no further. Finally, Forbes went to Dr. Armand Hammer, long the most favored capitalist in the communist world and, not just incidentally, the man who had managed to get clearance for the motorcycling expedition in the Soviet Union. Without apparent difficulty, Hammer managed to open the doors again.

Fun and firstness were not the only items on the agenda. Malcolm also hoped to make a unique contribution to Chinese sports through the journey. His plan was to give the balloon and three of the motorcycles he and his team would be using to the Chinese as presents at the end of the trip. He offered to teach Chinese athletes how to use the equipment for pleasure and competition and to invite a team of Chinese balloonists and motorcyclists to the West, all expenses paid, for further training.

The expedition was to have five members: Malcolm's twenty-nine-year-old son, Timothy, a filmmaker who has been riding motorcycles since he was a teenager; Cook Nielson, thirty-nine, a photographer, former editor of Cycle magazine and onetime motorcycle racer; Kip Cleland, the thirty-three-year-old Director of Fitness for this magazine (one of the more unusual titles in the generally unhealthy world of American journalism); Dennis Fleck, thirty-five, the Director, Balloon Ascension Division, Forbes magazine, indisputably the most unusual title in American journalism; finally there was myself, a thirty-one-year-old weekend motorcyclist and the chronicler of a number of eccentric expeditions. A five-man crew from Armand Hammer Productions would also be along to make a documentary film of the journey.

—Clifford D. May

China's Great Wall once snaked 2,000 miles through rugged mountains and across vast plains to guard the borders against barbarians to the north.

China · 149

As the official guests of China's Ministry of Sport and Culture, we would be the first Americans, in fact the first foreigners of any stripe or color, to tour China by motorcycle. We would also be the first people, Chinese included, to fly a hot-air balloon in the Middle Kingdom. In addition the trip would be a goodwill tour. As the innumerable cables traded back and forth during the planning put it, we would "promote the friendship and further understanding between our two peoples." Corny, perhaps, but true; it was definitely part of the mission.

We flew into Peking and were met by Mr. Chen Hanzhang, Mr. Cui Shuyi and several other representatives from the China Sports Service who would be our guides and companions. Early the next afternoon, we flew to Xi'an, the capital of Shaanxi Province in north central China.

Nurtured by the Wei River and protected by mountains to the south and east, Shaanxi was the cradle of Chinese civilization and the center of the Chinese world for nearly two millennia. It was also the site where the fabled Silk Route began, an overland caravan route that formed the first and for hundreds of years the only link between China and the West. As we drove up to the Shaanxi Guest House and saw five gleaming orange and black Harleys lined up in the parking lot, it occurred to Cliff that Xi'an was indeed an appropriate point to begin our journey.

The next morning at breakfast we were given the most precious souvenir of the trip: Chinese drivers' licenses. A couple of the younger Chinese with us seemed as interested in them as we were. Unless you work as a driver in China, one of them explained, getting a license is a rare privilege. And, one of the others added, if you're privileged enough to get one, you probably already have a driver and don't need a license anyway; there are no private cars at all.

That day we were to take an excursion to a series of 2,000-year-old tombs a couple of hours' ride from Xi'an. The road leaving town was surprisingly good, well paved but a bit narrower than a secondary road in the U.S. There was no mistaking, however, that this was not

the United States. Crowding the road ahead were bicycles, donkey carts, peasants hauling loads, some small two-wheeled tractors pulling wagonloads of brick, and convoys of very dark green trucks. The police cleared our way through this dense and motley assortment of traffic, but I couldn't help wondering what it would've been like without them—dodging a truck while it passes a tractor that's dodging a bicycle passing an overburdened burro.

A youngster tries on a Harley.

Curious onlookers lined the roads much of the way.

Out of pavement in Shaanxi Providence.

Arriving at our destination, we passed a long row of people hawking souvenirs. Nothing extraordinary about that—but this was China, land of official Friendship Stores and government-owned department stores. And these folks, their goods displayed on makeshift tables, didn't look a bit official. As we walked by, they enthusiastically waved their wares in the air, beckoning us to check them out. As it turned out, these people were part of an experiment which allowed certain individuals to work for their own profit; it was one of a series of recent reforms intended to increase the nation's productivity.

In the afternoon, we returned to Xi'an to inflate the balloon in the sports stadium there. The weather was perfect for ballooning—clear skies and a gentle breeze. As the sixty-foot-tall multicolored orb rose into the air, the Chinese were spellbound. Everyone loves a balloon; it made a perfect vehicle to salute the rediscovered friendship between Chinese and Americans. After giving several tethered rides to local officials, my father asked if he could now go for a free flight. The Chinese happily agreed. So with Denny and Mr. Cui on board and the film cameraman hanging precariously from a harness attached to the crown of the balloon, they took off. As they floated over the perimeter of the stadium, Mr. Chen came over to me and said, "It's very beautiful. Tell them to come back now, please." The other Chinese smiled and nodded. I explained that they couldn't come back; a balloon, you see, goes with the wind. Their smiles gave way to looks of confusion and consternation.

Into a Red Flag limousine I was escorted, and off we raced in pursuit. We spotted the balloon in a field a few miles from the stadium. Apparently, we weren't the only ones to see it. By the time we arrived on the scene, literally thousands of startled locals had gathered to get a closer look at this strange vehicle and welcome the white-faced foreigners who climbed out of it. The distress of Mr. Chen and the others at learning the meaning of "free flight" seemed to

(RIGHT) Xi'an witnessed the first free flight in China. The field was empty when the balloon landed, but within minutes hundreds had gathered. Inset top: TV Cameraman Kevin O'Brien hangs precariously from a harness to get a novel angle.

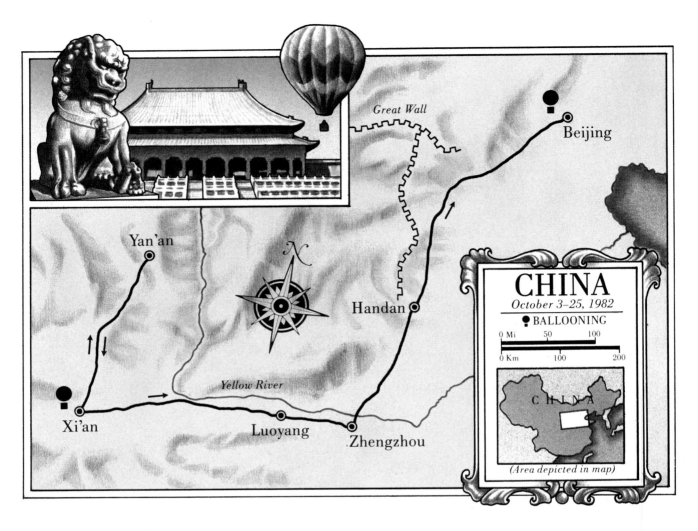

have gone; their smiles had returned. But I smelled trouble.

As we gathered in the parking lot Friday morning, my father was told that, unfortunately, the propane gas in this region was of poor quality. So out of concern for our safety, there'd be no more ballooning. The discussion that ensued gave us our first taste of the Chinese method of saying no. It seems it was a matter of manners. Our hosts would approach an issue obliquely, offering a plausible excuse —preferably one which was unavoidable and beyond anyone's control. Hence, the bad gas. The Chinese understand this, accepting the excuse gracefully, while realizing it simply means "No." But we were Americans, and, besides, my father is rarely known to take no without a struggle. Wasn't it his persistence, after all, that got us to China in the first place? Even-

tually, the Chinese understood this and promised to get the tanks filled with "good" propane as soon as it could be found.

We left the guest house and began our journey in earnest. With Xi'an and its besmogged air behind us, we rode north into flat farm country. The fields were alive with activity as hardworking peasants harvested crops and made ready for a new planting. In one, I saw four women straining to pull a plow. More often, yoked oxen performed this grueling chore, but this wouldn't be the only time I saw people pulling plows. On the road, we would pass many farm tractors hauling wagons loaded with bricks, gravel and, occasionally, produce, but

The Big Goose Pagoda. Dating from the 7th century, the 240 foot tower offers a spectacular panorama of the surrounding countryside. Getting to the top takes many steps.

Carts—usually mule-drawn, sometimes man-drawn —outnumbered trucks and tractors on the roads.

Camping beneath the oldest tree in China at the Tomb of the Yellow Emperor.

only once did I see one used in a field to pull a plow. On the farm in China everything is done by raw animal strength, human or otherwise.

We were now entering an area where no Americans had been since the Revolution in 1948, and where a motorcycle gang had certainly never ventured before. As we approached the first fair-sized town, we began to realize just what that meant.

Lining the street and jamming an overpass up ahead must have been a few thousand people. The whole town had turned out to greet us! I have no idea what they'd been told to expect or what they must have thought of six leather-clad Americans on five Harleys flying the Chinese and American flags, but as we rode by they applauded; when we waved back, they broke into fits of laughter. We were the circus come to town.

We spent the night in tents pitched beneath the oldest tree in China on the grounds of the

156

Shaanxi Province. Alerted we'd be passing through, whole towns turned out to greet the Forbes caravan in Shaanxi Province.

Tomb of the Yellow Emperor. Legend has it that the tree was planted by China's first Emperor himself some five thousand years ago. And, we were told, sleeping beneath it would assure us of a long life.

We were awakened early the next morning by the improbable strains of "The East Is Red" booming from the loudspeakers of a nearby commune. Public address systems reach 80 percent of China's population, broadcasting music, announcements and news.

We continued north through broken, hilly countryside reminiscent of the Badlands of South Dakota. But here it is all under cultivation, the hills terraced into wedding-cake-like tiers.

As we wound through the canyons and across the dusty, windswept mesas, Kip and Denny pulled up alongside me. Grinning from ear to ear, Kip pointed to the tall weeds growing by the roadside—marijuana! A little farther on, I noticed a grizzled old man bending under the weight of a tremendous bundle of the stuff. For the next few hours, we passed mile upon mile of it. No, the Chinese don't smoke it; they use it to make rope.

Our destination was Yan'an, a town of about 70,000 people and considered by the Chinese to be the cradle of their revolution. In 1934, Mao and 100,000 Communist guerrillas were forced to retreat from Jiangin Province in the south of China by Chiang Kai-shek's Nationalist army. Known as the Long March, the retreat ended two years and six thousand miles later, when Mao and the 8,000 guerrillas who'd survived arrived in Yan'an. The rugged country we'd been riding through the last day and a half formed a nearly impenetrable natural barrier to the pursuing Nationalists. The dwellings in the hills of Yan'an served as Mao's headquarters until 1947. When we wandered through them later, I found it incredible to imagine that the world's largest revolution had been planned and directed in such humble circumstances.

China · 157

Yan'an. Carved from the rugged hills on the banks of the Yen Shui river and known as the cradle of the revolution, the city served as Mao's headquarters from 1936 to 1947. The world's largest revolution was directed from cave dwellings cut in the hillsides.

That afternoon we again put up the balloon. True to their word, our hosts had managed to procure propane of "suitable quality" somewhere along the way. But there was no question of a free flight. The hills would have made it impossible anyway, but that was not the only reason. "The problem is security," Mr. Cui had revealed earlier. "Some of the people from state security objected." The large crowd in Yan'an, however, delighted in watching the tethered balloon bob up and down in the stadium. When my father gave a ride to a group of children, everyone broke into wild applause.

Monday morning we headed back toward Xi'an, back through the same worn, cultivated countryside. Along the way, we saw what seemed an apt emblem of China today. One night in Yijun, a dusty coal-mining town, Cook and I wandered around with Mr. Yu, a representative of Occidental in China who'd been accompanying us. There were no street lamps and except for the headlights of an occasional truck, the town was completely dark. We entered the one shop still open and found it was a tiny restaurant run by an old woman. It was already quite late by Chinese standards and hardly anyone was there, so I asked how late she stayed open. "Midnight," was the reply. I was puzzled. "Who," I wondered, "would come in so late?" She pointed to a truck driver who'd just come in. This restaurant was a Chinese truck stop, and this old woman and her family had been in business about nine months—another experiment in private enterprise. I was no less startled to find she paid a mere 8 percent in taxes. She seemed appalled when I told her businesses in America pay as much as 50 percent to our government. Cook and I wished her luck and left, musing that the Chinese Communists appeared to understand the meaning of "incentive" better than the American government.

Our 400-plus-mile dogleg from Xi'an to Yan'an to Qin completed, we now headed east on the road to Peking. We'd been in China just over a week and had come to know a little of our Chinese hosts and they a little of us. Mr. Cui, the first Chinese to ride on the back of a Harley and to fly in a hot-air balloon, had proven to be a dauntless and delightful soul. His stiffly formal English belied a warm heart and thoughtful mind. Mr. Chen, hardworking

Aloft, the Friendship Balloon never failed to bring smiles to the faces below.

and dignified, had done everything in his power to accommodate us and smooth our way. Indeed, throughout the trip we were shown nothing but the most gracious hospitality. But behind these personalities was a bureaucracy as vast as it was rigid. Every mile of the trip and every hour of our days had been meticulously planned. Any deviation caused considerable dismay. Our hosts were responsible for us, and they were intent on putting us through the paces without a hitch. The flexibility which we, as Americans, took for granted was not part of their world.

Around noon a light rain began to fall. Despite it, large crowds still lined the streets of the villages. Everywhere, our caravan had been greeted with the excitement of a circus come to town. Here, in our baggy, bright yellow rain gear, we now even looked the part.

It was still raining as we left Shaanxi Province. At the border, we thanked our Shaanxi guides for the fabulous time and bid them farewell. Then our new escorts took us eastward into Henan Province and slowly toward Sanmenxia.

The country turned flat again. But unlike the dusty dry brown of Shaanxi, here it was green. Around noon we arrived in Luoyang, another ancient center of Chinese culture. After lunch, we rode to the Longmen Caves, a series of more than 1,000 grottoes on the Yi River which house

In yellow rain suits and full-face helmets, the Capitalists Tools resembled ducks from outer space—and undoubtedly appear no less alien to this family on the road in Henan Province. (RIGHT) Mobility for the masses. Row upon row of bicycles jam a Xi'an parking lot. Bicycles are to Chinese what cars are to Americans.

the carved statues and reliefs of nearly 100,000 Buddhas. Many were missing heads and arms, the inevitable result, I assumed, of time. Not entirely so. One of our guides explained that during the Cultural Revolution gangs of youths reveled in randomly knocking a head off here, an arm there as a gesture of continuous revolution. The Buddhas, however, represented only a small part of the destruction wrought by the Cultural Revolution—which the Party leadership and virtually all the Chinese we met now consider a national tragedy of vast proportions.

162 · Around the World on Hot Air & Two Wheels

关羽

Putting Luoyang behind us the next morning, we saw the countryside change again. It now reminded me of parts of the American West— southern Colorado and New Mexico. Despite the wide expanses, we all began to feel vaguely oppressed. Cliff later put it this way: "There were no fallow fields, no wild forests; everything had been touched and retouched by man. No matter how deep into the back country we went we never felt we were getting back to nature or away from civilization."

A day later we arrived in Zhengzhou, the pro-

vincial capital, well before noon. At lunch my father was told a message had arrived from Peking: his meeting with China's Prime Minister had been pushed a day ahead. To make it on time, it was suggested, we should park the bikes here and take the train back to Peking—after we had toured another temple and a handicraft factory in the afternoon, that is. Understand that sightseeing has never been high on my father's list of favorite pastimes. He enjoys touring on bikes precisely because he sees more of the country and people. Pop balked at the suggestion of another temple-and-handicraft-factory tour. He explained that we had come to China to ride motorcycles and fly the balloon. The train was out of the question, and rather than visit the sights we would spend the afternoon flying the balloon. After lunch, when he was told in the usual indirect way that flying the balloon wasn't possible, he decided we should then move on to the next stop, a commune where, we'd been told days before, we could fly. The result was a fierce contest of wills: Pop versus Henan Province security authorities—with our translator, the dauntless Mr. Cui, caught in the middle.

Mr. Cui: "The commune doesn't expect us today."

My father: "Then we can camp out in the tents."

"Please, Mr. Forbes, go to the rooms and rest and have a cup of tea."

"We've only traveled eighty kilometers today. We're not tired."

"But we have to cross the Yalu River, and we have to make arrangements with the bridge in advance."

"Come on, Mr. Cui. Let's just go to the commune. There's no problem. It's just that if we can't do what we came here to do, we should move on. That's all."

So it went back and forth, until Mr. Cui finally gave up and disappeared with his colleagues into the guest house.

We waited in the parking lot for Mr. Cui to return. Fifteen minutes, thirty minutes, an hour. It was getting late, and Pop began to think about fallback positions. It now seemed quite possible that the Chinese might simply refuse to let us go on. Around four-thirty Mr. Cui finally emerged and told us the arrangements had been made.

We left Zhengzhou and made our way to the commune, crossing the Yalu River around sundown.

Unfortunately, there was to be no ballooning the next morning. The Chinese were obliging, but the wind was not. So we hit the road again and headed out of Henan Province and into Hobei. While no trees had yet turned, fall was

At Luoyang stadium hundreds of children turned out to see the Friendship Balloon inflated. Though high winds brought disappointment on that score, instant pictures brought smiles.

Sports Service, and Miss Li, a journalist for the Sports Service News, who had come to cover our arrival in Peking the next day. On the way, we had a discussion about the sexual mores in China and the U.S. I asked George if he had a girlfriend. He did; they've been going together for two years. But I discovered that in China when unmarried couples say good night, they mean exactly that.

"When you say good night, what do you do?"

"We shake hands."

I was incredulous, but he insisted that they had never even kissed. I looked over at Miss Li, who nodded approvingly. I suspected George was saying this for her benefit, but I'll never know for sure. In any case, to speak of the relations between the sexes in China is to raise a subject more touchy than even Communist Ideology.

That evening a banquet was given in our honor by the Vice Governor of Hobei Province. In practically every town we'd visited, no matter how humble its circumstances, we had been treated to delicious ten-course feasts: Peking duck, quail eggs, dried pork, roast chicken, fried sweet potatoes, rice cakes, dumplings, crisp lotus root, sea slugs and other local deli-

headed south and was suddenly struck by an odd thought: I hadn't seen a bird since coming to China—and we'd now covered nearly 1,000 miles. Birds have a bad habit it seems: They eat seeds. In the 1950s there had been a program to eliminate the "Four Pests": rats, flies, mosquitoes and sparrows. It was highly successful.

We were now covering more ground, and after another guest house and another failed attempt to fly the balloon, we arrived in Shijiazhuang, capital of Hobei. Our hosts suggested a trip to Long Xing monastery. I was the only taker.

I was surprised and somewhat embarrassed to see a Red Flag limousine waiting for me. But I climbed in along with "George," one of the younger Chinese representatives from the

China · 165

"THE FACES OF CHINA."

cacies. Between courses, there were innumerable toasts to "the friendship and understanding between our two peoples" made with small glasses of mao tai—a fiery Chinese liquor which Cliff aptly described as being to a dry martini what a Harley is to a bicycle.

The Vice Governor was a crusty, jovial man with a great capacity for mao tai. Each toast (and since it was our last night on the road there were even more than usual) concluded with the same refrain: "Gambei!"—"Bottoms Up!"

Weary but exultant, frustrated by what we hadn't done and brimming over with the experiences we'd had, we entered Peking. On five of Harley's finest, we rode down broad avenues past Mao's mausoleum and the Forbidden City. We posed for official photos with the bikes in T'ien An Mien square, then moved on to the Peking Hotel and a well-earned rest.

The next morning we accompanied Dr. Armand Hammer, who was in Peking on business, to meet Chinese Prime Minister Zhao Ziyang. My father presented Prime Minister Zhao with

one of our red vests and a balloon pin making him an honorary member of the team, which he laughingly put on. Pop pinned on his tunic the emblem of our China/U.S. Friendship Balloon, with its crossed China/U.S. flags.

Then we were off on the Harleys to visit China's most famous landmark: the Great Wall. To our great pleasure the well-paved road wound sharply through precipitous hills.

We were not going merely to visit the Wall; we were going to inflate the balloon next to it. But the winds were high on the ridge of the mountains where the Wall stands. My father combed the area for a windbreak, but gusts swirled from every direction. It was growing late and Pop was determined not to let the opportunity pass, so the balloon was readied in a small parking lot. The breeze was still stiff as the fans filled the envelope. Pop struggled to control the basket as he lit the burners. Kip, Denny and several Chinese rushed around checking the tether lines as the wind buffeted the balloon first this way and then that. Sud-

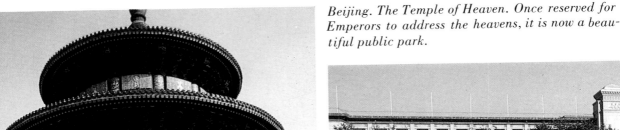

Beijing. The Temple of Heaven. Once reserved for Emperors to address the heavens, it is now a beautiful public park.

The team logo: *"Forbes Hails China-U.S. Amity."* Translated directly the Chinese for Forbes means Lucky Rags.

福布斯杂志
欢呼中美友谊

The Capitalist Tools in T'ien An Men Square at the end of their journey.

MSF makes Chinese Premier Zhao Ziyang an honory member of the Team as Dr. Armand Hammer, who opened the door for the trip, looks on.

denly, as if yielding to Pop's will, the wind died; the balloon rose gently to the end of its tethers.

That evening Dr. Hammer hosted a banquet in my father's honor, an epic affair of seventeen courses served to hundreds of guests in a tremendous ornately decorated hall. Chinese singers and dancers entertained us, and a few dozen musicians played charming renditions of "Oh, Susanna," "Dixie" and other American favorites. And, of course, there were speeches and toasts to friendship. In the elevator on the way to our rooms after the banquet, my father said that he had asked permission for a free flight tomorrow but was denied. The security police simply wouldn't allow it. "But," he said, "what if tomorrow when we are giving rides on the tether . . . what if the knots slip and we float away?"

The weather was perfect when we arrived at the field the next morning. Pleased and slightly nervous, Mr. Chen introduced us to some of the officials who had turned out to see the display, including his immediate boss, Mr. Yuan, the deputy manager of the Sports Service and the Minister of Sports and Culture. The Vice Provost of the Institute then told my father, "No one has seen anything like this before. We look forward to a good performance."

"We hope we can give you one." My father smiled.

China · 169

After giving several tethered rides to the delighted bureaucrats, Kip and Denny loaded a fresh propane tank. As arranged the night before, Cliff climbed on board. While still on the ground, Kip offhandedly began to untie the knots. Mr. Chen suddenly realized what was going on. "What are you doing? No free flight! Not allowed!" he exclaimed. Several people grabbed hold of the basket.

The vehemence of their reaction surprised me. Though I knew they had to say my father couldn't fly, I'd hoped it would be a pro forma shake of the head accompanied by a knowing wink. I'd hoped that by now Mr. Chen and the others would understand. But we were in China, and even if they had wanted to, they couldn't. It was the Chinese theory of accountability. Just as they were responsible for our safety on the bikes, they would be held responsible if we broke the rules. Okay, I figured, you can't fight the Great Hall of The People, even if you're Malcolm Forbes.

At Pop's request, Cliff hopped out of the basket and Pop asked if there was anyone else who should have a ride. A young woman, the javelin-throwing champion of the Institute, was presented. The knots were retied and the balloon lifted off carrying the javelin thrower, Kip, Denny and Pop skyward. Within seconds, the tether lines "slipped" and they were free. "No free flight! No free flight!" Mr. Chen cried out in vain. The javelin thrower innocently waved back.

As they floated off in the distance, a white-faced Mr. Chen turned to me. In a sad, distraught tone, he said, "We trusted you." As I looked at this utterly disconsolate man, I felt that we had indeed betrayed him. I realized then that he saw his whole career floating away with the friendship balloon. The only thing I could think to do was get the balloon down as quickly as possible. So I ran off to find Cook, who had the walkie-talkie with him.

"Denny? Can you hear me? Come in. Over." Cook, holding the walkie-talkie expectantly, heard nothing but static. The Chinese gathered around us grew more agitated by the minute.

Cook: "Denny, where are you? Over."

Finally, Denny responded. "Uh, I don't

know, Cook. But there are about ten cannons pointing straight at us."

The transmission then broke up. Had he really said that?

The Chinese then led Cook off to a car. They didn't explain why. Thinking we might all be headed to jail, or God knows what, I decided I'd better go with him. We climbed into the car and were relieved to see just Mr. Chen and Mr. Yu. Mr. Yu took over the walkie-talkie, and we drove off in the general direction of the balloon. When we reestablished radio contact, we found they had landed at an Army base some miles from the Institute.

At the base a host of Red Army troops had gathered around the balloon. Despite this being a restricted zone—off limits to foreigners and Chinese citizens alike—we saw no trace of hostility or suspicion. The javelin thrower, still

The Friendship Balloon "slipped" its tether in Beijing and floated away while anxious officials cried, "No free flight!" On landing in an artillery range at a Red Army base after the unauthorized flight, the balloon was quickly surrounded. But the troops there, like the Chinese encountered throughout the trip, were hospitable, curious and helpful.

170

"Gambei! Cheers!" MSF and Li Menghua, Minister of Sport and Culture, toast the "tether line" of friendship.

smiling happily, was led off, and with the aid of the troops, we packed up the balloon.

Mr. Chen then introduced us to the base commander. After my father pinned a balloon pin on his Mao jacket and Cook took a few pictures, we were taken to a reception room and offered tea. They told us that a general, the commander of the Peking Military District, was coming out to meet us.

While we sat, sipping tea, one by one the Chinese excused themselves and disappeared, leaving us alone in the room with a portrait of Chairman Mao staring sternly down at us (outside of his mausoleum, this was the only portrait of the Great Helmsman we'd seen in an official setting). We had assumed that Denny and Kip would be joining us once the balloon had been loaded onto the truck, but after an hour they still hadn't shown.

We could overhear intense telephone conversations coming from a nearby office, and we began to suspect that the general wasn't coming at all and that we were being held while our hosts figured out how to handle the situation. Then, without any comment about the flight or the mysterious general, we were sent back to

the Institute. From there we headed back to the hotel, still uncertain of the outcome.

That evening, as planned, we were feted by the Ministry of Sport and Culture in the Great Hall of The People. Everyone appeared cordial and when the Minister of Sport and Culture made his toast, he never even alluded to the day's goings-on. My father responded by thanking the Chinese and explaining that the government had taken a risk in allowing us to come as part of their effort to understand America and Americans. With a nod to the still-nervous Mr. Chen, he went on to emphasize that none of our Chinese companions knew anything about the free flight. He continued: "What we did today, it wasn't to be naughty or unfriendly. It was to demonstrate the sport of ballooning. A balloon is not meant to be tied down. It's part of the wind. It's a beautiful thing to see—if you're not with the security section of the Ministry of Foreign Affairs." I happened to have had a director from said ministry on my left, and I was greatly relieved to find him laughing. My father concluded: "The balloon is now yours, your responsibility. If it flies in the wrong place, you must answer for that. One day, I hope, China will be among the champions in the sport. As far as the friendship between our countries goes, nothing can break that tether line, not even an unauthorized free flight."

The applause that followed led me to believe that though perhaps the Chinese would never really understand us, they had accepted and even come to respect us. We certainly felt that way of them.

And, as Cliff May wrote:

The end of a long journey is always a melancholy time. Perhaps that is another reason why, at the close of the motorcycle expedition to the Soviet Union nearly three years ago, Malcolm began contemplating this venture. Perhaps all journeys begin not with a single step but with a craving for the tingle that only anticipation can create.

Shortly before our departure from China, Malcolm receives a midnight telephone call from Dr. Armand Hammer. He says he is with General Mohammad Zia ul-Haq, the Pakistani leader, and that the two of them have been talk-

Looking down from the Great Wall onto the parking lot where the Friendship Balloon was inflated. (LEFT) Surprisingly, portraits of the Great Helmsman, Mao Tse-tung, were seen only twice in official settings during the trip. Here at Beijing's Gate of Heavenly Peace and in a reception room at a Red Army base.

ing about Malcolm. Dr. Hammer says that Malcolm should get out of bed and put on some clothes: Zia wants to meet him. A limousine is on its way. After the introductions have been made, Zia says that Malcolm's expedition must have been very exciting. But he wonders if Malcolm is aware that Pakistan is also a fascinating country, a country that no one has ever explored by motorcycle and balloon. "No one?" Malcolm asks. "Then we'd be the first?" The temptation sounded too good to resist.

China · 173

The pagoda forest at the fabled Shaolin Monastery, birthplace of Zen Buddhism, in Henan Province. Each of the pagodas contains the remains of a monk who was respected for his wisdom.

8

CHAPTER

PAKISTAN

Clifford D. May

IN THE SMALL, DARK HOURS of an early April morning, Malcolm Forbes and several members of the world's only international goodwill motorcycle gang found themselves disembarking from a Boeing 747 in Karachi, the populous Pakistani city on the shores of the Arabian Sea. The air was warm and humid, heavy with smells both sweet and acrid, odors of growth and of decay. As spotlights illuminated the wrinkles on their blue blazers and television cameras recorded the smiles on their drawn faces, they were led into a large room dominated by ornately patterned carpets, brass tables, carved wooden doors and crystal chandeliers.

A delegation of dignified gentlemen was there to greet them. Some of these men wore Western-style suits, some wore crisply tailored military uniforms, others wore baggy trousers and loose shirts extending to their knees, the tradi-

Smiling kids after landing in a field outside Peshawar. (BELOW) Curious onlookers await the Team's arrival to inflate the Minar-e-Pakistan *balloon in Lahore. Welcome banners were hung throughout the city, where the real Minar stands.*

tional garb of the region. Tea and soft drinks were proffered as members of the local press corps posed their questions. Essentially, they boiled down to these: Why had this team come to Pakistan? What did they hope to accomplish? What was the meaning behind this not-very-grownup passion for motorcycles and balloons?

Malcolm shook off his exhaustion and endeavored to explain. There's no better way to view a country than from atop a motorcycle, he said. On a motorcycle you don't just see the environment, you integrate with it. You feel the temperature change from mountain to valley. You smell the crops in the fields. You're alert to what's going on around you because motorcyclists who do not stay alert tend to have very short careers.

As for balloons, he continued, that was how man first fulfilled the dream of flight in 1783.

And ballooning remains today the most beautiful, the most peaceful, the most gentle way to leave the earth. What better way to celebrate the bicentennial of ballooning than by introducing the sport to yet another country? At the conclusion of this trip, he said, a hot-air balloon and all the equipment and training necessary would be provided so that Pakistani athletes could begin ballooning for fun and competition.

Finally, Malcolm noted that Pakistan is a nation much admired in the West these days for the courage and strength it has shown in providing a haven for the continuing flood of refugees from the ugly war northwest of the border.

All that was accurate, of course, and it seemed to satisfy our interrogators. But it also served to disguise the fact that, like most Americans, we really knew remarkably little about this country of 84 million precariously poised among such volatile neighbors as Afghanistan, Iran, the Soviet Union, China and, of course,

Conditions are primitive in the rural areas of Pakistan. For example, buffalo are still a mainstay of the farm economy. But this Moslem nation of 84 million is proud and fiercely independent.

Birdcages in the bazaar at Peshawar.

India, from which Pakistan was carved in 1947 as a homeland for the subcontinent's Muslim population.

The position of this land within a vortex of struggle and change is more than just a current event: Alexander the Great fought his

Our message in Urdu.

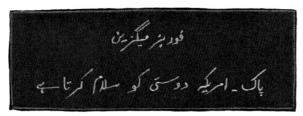

way into the territory, as did Timur the Lame and Genghis Khan. The British were here, and before them came the Moghuls; the Arabs invaded, and before them the Buddhists; Aryans lived here, too, and centuries prior to their arrival there was the Indus Valley civilization, a great and complex culture that flourished at a time when Europeans were still huddling in dank caves. Just the names on the map convey a sense of the region's exotic, intriguing past: the Punjab, the Sind, the Khyber Pass, the Valley of Swat, the Vale of Peshawar, the Karakorum, the Himalayas, Hunza.

It should also be revealed that the appearance of Malcolm and the Gang in Pakistan at this particular time had come about thanks largely to another name, hardly less redolent of exoticism and intrigue. In Peking last autumn, near the conclusion of the Capitalist Tool motorcycle-and-balloon expedition through China, transnational industrialist Armand Hammer had introduced Malcolm Forbes to the visiting Pakistani leader, General Mohammad Zia ul-Haq. In the course of the conversation that followed, General Zia suggested that Malcolm might be interested in bringing his Harley-Davidson-and-hot-air-balloon caravan to Pakistan for another journey of exploration and adventure.

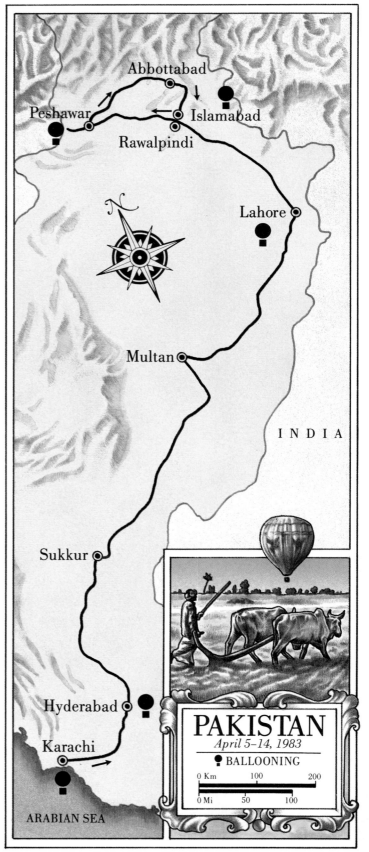

PAKISTAN
April 5–14, 1983
BALLOONING

180 · Around the World on Hot Air & Two Wheels

Malcolm eagerly accepted and, as a way of saying thanks, promised to build Pakistan a special gift balloon and to train a team of Pakistani athletes in its use. He approached the well-known British balloonmaker Don Cameron and asked him to construct an inflatable flying machine in the likeness of the Minar-e-Pakistan, the country's independence monument situated in the ancient city of Lahore. Cameron took Malcolm literally: The balloon he built was almost an exact replica of the Minar, itself a long, narrow structure, a sort of Asiatic version of the Eiffel Tower.

At 240 feet, the *Minar* was the tallest balloon ever built, a huge sleeve of air with precious little lifting power. It was suggested that Malcolm and his team come to Pakistan in April, normally the driest month of the year. That meant there would not be time enough for Cameron to test the balloon before shipping it. The *Minar*'s first flight—assuming it was capable of flight—would have to be in Pakistan.

The Team poses before the Minar-e-Pakistan monument to the nation's independence.

The Capitalist Tools rumble through a small town on the road to Multan.

One last unknown focused on how the Pakistani people would regard this group of hell-bent-for-leather Americans. After all, the country is officially known as the Islamic Republic of Pakistan. In the neighboring Islamic republic of Iran, Americans nowadays are held in about as much esteem as bubonic rodents. And only four years ago the American embassy in the Pakistani capital of Islamabad was stormed by a furious mob, incensed over reports—which turned out to be erroneous—that Washington had been involved in the seizure of the Grand Mosque in Mecca. Perhaps times and attitudes had changed since then. Perhaps not.

The team Malcolm assembled for the expedition was composed of many of the same hard-driving motorcyclists that had crossed China in the fall. There was son Timothy, a documentary filmmaker (whose newlywed wife, Anne, understood the priorities that dictated that they spend their honeymoon half a world apart). There was Dennis Fleck, director of the Balloon Ascension Division of Forbes, Inc.; and Kip Cleland, the magazine's director of physical fitness.

Two team members who had not been along for the ride in China were James Summers, a twenty-three-year-old ex-Green Beret who served as Malcolm's bodyguard and personal assistant; and Barry Coleman, a British journalist who has long specialized in just about every aspect of motorcycling.

Finally, there was me, a veteran of the Long Ride in China, an incurable motorcyclist and itinerant journalist on a busman's holiday.

Malcolm was understandably anxious to find out whether his great balloon was or was not a

Pakistan · 181

white elephant. So just hours after the press conference, the pale light of dawn found us moving through the hectic streets of Karachi en route to the old horse-race grounds, where we hoped to inaugurate the *Minar* later in the day. A city of nearly 4 million and the commercial center of the country, Karachi seemed a confusing welter of modern office buildings and cinder-block slums, browning palm trees and graying billboards inscribed with such slogans as: "Yummy Ice Cream—It's the Yummiest" and "Eagle Is the Best, Beats the Rest."

Toyotas and Mercedes-Benzes weaved through columns of motorized rickshaws, donkey carts and heavily burdened camels wearing bells on their knees and haughty expressions on their snouts.

By the time we returned to the race course after lunch it was already packed with several thousand spectators, all eager to see the historic first flight of the world's biggest balloon. A breeze was beginning to "freshen," as Malcolm put it, and Denny was harboring doubts about whether the launching should be attempted un-

less it died down. But Malcolm was determined to give it a shot.

The long tube was laid out on the dusty ground, and two motorized fans filled it with air. That done, Malcolm climbed into the overturned gondola and hit the trigger on the propane burner, tickling the throat of the balloon with long feathers of flame. Nothing happened. Then, very slowly, the balloon began to rise. Or rather, half of it did: The end far from the flame was not hot enough; it remained hovering just above the ground so that the balloon ascended with a crick in the middle, a bend that soon developed into a full right angle, giving the balloon the appearance of a great broken finger.

The wind gathered force and, as it did, hope that the *Minar* might straighten up and fly right vanished. Not this afternoon, anyway. Disappointment etched into his face, Malcolm called for the *Minar*'s deflation, and at the same time, he ordered the crew to lay out a second balloon

Inflating the full-size replica—the tallest balloon ever built—required some improvisation.

While the aeronauts heat the balloon from the inside, local volunteers hold down the end to ensure that when loosened it has enough buoyancy to rise to its full height.

brought along as a backup: the ten-year-old *Dream of Flight*, a conventionally shaped balloon lavishly illustrated with figures from Greek mythology that are associated with flying.

The *Dream of Flight* balloon inflated quickly as the crowd applauded in approval. But then the wind strengthened further, so much so that the balloon began to strain against its single tether. Malcolm decided against attempting a free flight. Instead, he executed a swift and rough descent smack on top of the *Minar*.

The crowd seemed amused by the performance. "Well, it was a small failure, but at least you tried," one man told me. Another spectator, identifying himself as an engineer, suggested that the only way we would ever be able to raise the ungainly *Minar* would be by attaching another balloon to its nose and raising that section first. "This balloon, it is far too tall," he explained. "It is the law of physics. With that shape it is not going to fly without help."

We rose early on Wednesday morning eager to begin the first leg of our overland trip, head-ing northwest through the vast Sind desert. Following after our motorcycle caravan in a minibus were three Pakistanis who would soon become our friends as well as our guides. There was Zakir Hussain Syed—we called him Zach—representing the Ministry of Tourism, a large man, as genial as a favorite uncle, an efficient but never officious organizer who managed to retain his unruffled, debonair bearing under the most harrying of conditions. There was Lieutenant Colonel Mohammad Akram Khan, a true officer and gentleman, wiry and stoic, a born leader whom any one of us would have willingly followed into battle. An instructor in "physical training and mountain warfare," the colonel represented the "Adventure Foundation (Pakistan)," a nonprofit organization in the Outward Bound tradition and the outfit that would be undertaking to spread the gospel of ballooning

Pakistan · 183

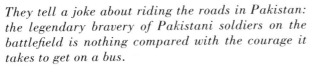

They tell a joke about riding the roads in Pakistan: the legendary bravery of Pakistani soldiers on the battlefield is nothing compared with the courage it takes to get on a bus.

after Malcolm's departure. Finally, there was Muhammad Nadeem Anwar, a bright and amiable twenty-three-year-old engineer and aspiring balloonist, also a member of the Adventure Foundation.

Expecting a long morning ride through arid countryside, I applied a goodly coating of gooey sunscreen to my face. And predictably enough, by seven-thirty the rain had begun, a steady downpour that quickly coated the roads with a thick film of oil, mud and water. The only sights for us to enjoy were the patterns formed by the raindrops on our visors.

The sun reemerged from behind the clouds as we were passing the city of Hyderabad. A green pickup truck containing a contingent of police escorts joined us and led the way. Standing in the flatbed, the policemen waved the oncoming trucks, buses, cars and carts to one side or the other, helping to speed us along our route. They were a friendly, jovial bunch, these Pakistani policemen, and they seemed to be enjoying the break from their routine.

They had been riding with us for only about forty-five minutes when the accident occurred.

From my place near the end of the line of motorcycles, I couldn't see it happen, but I did hear the sound of the impact, and I soon saw the bus sliding to a halt on the shoulder of the road. The driver of the bus had seen the police too late and had hit his brakes too hard on a stretch of pavement littered with squashed oranges. The bus had skidded and sideswiped the pickup.

By the time we dismounted from our bikes, the three policemen were on their backs by the curbside, pained and glassy looks in their eyes. Our Pakistani colleagues helped them remove their shoes and loosen their collars. Before long, an ambulance arrived to collect them.

Their injuries turned out to be less serious than we had feared. One policeman had broken

his arm; the others were merely bruised and in shock. But it was an inauspicious start to the journey, and it left us all feeling nervous and vulnerable.

As the hours wore on, the air became increasingly dry and hot. The road was narrow and crowded with camels and donkeys and the now familiar Pakistani buses, with both passengers and luggage piled on the roof, and garishly decorated with hammered metal cartoon drawings of fighter planes and ocean liners and such disconcerting slogans as: "Ask forgiveness for your sins; this could be your final journey."

Even more ornate were the Pakistani trucks, nearly all of which had been customized with oversized cabs crowned by blunt prows and with a colorful mosaic of paintings paneling their sides. The paintings fell into four categories: those depicting beauty, usually in the

The trucks and buses are brightly decorated with hammered metal, elaborate designs and slogans offering such good advice as "Ask forgiveness for your sins; this could be your final journey." Bottom: The Minar-e-Pakistan is a particularly popular decorative motif.

form of a pretty girl; those that signified power, generally symbolized by a wild animal such as a tiger; those representing nature, for example, a landscape; and occasionally a tribute to a leader, a portrait of General Zia, for instance. The gaudier the truck or bus, evidently, the more business it attracts.

With so much traffic to contend with, our progress was frustratingly slow. Perhaps it was impatience, perhaps it was just bad luck that caused the second accident of the day. But as we entered a village around four o'clock, a small but stout donkey leapt into the path of Jim's bike and the two collided with a painful, percussive thud. Jim skidded off into the dust, barely managing to keep his heavy bike from tumbling over. As for the donkey, he stumbled off morosely, apparently planning to survive.

By the time we reached the Inter Pak Inn, a rest house by a reservoir outside Sukkur where we were to pass the night, we had been on the road for a full twelve hours. Yet in that time we had covered only about three hundred miles. I could hardly stay awake through dinner and retired to my room immediately afterward. Sleep came quickly and it lasted until the cock's crow just before dawn.

At nine o'clock we had already been on the road for several hours and were entering the Punjab, the biggest and most populated of Pakistan's provinces. Punjab means "land of five rivers," and as we moved northward the extensively irrigated land grew gradually greener.

The dwellings we passed were simple, mostly made of sun-dried mud, or adobe. They blended so completely with the ground beneath them that they seemed to be growing directly from the soil. The people who lived in these huts were poor, but it was poverty of a kind they have endured for generations. Certainly, they did not appear to be starving or desperate. And they seemed to find us diverting. They waved, smiled and applauded as we passed and approached us curiously whenever we would stop.

In every hardscrabble village, the most colorful structure was invariably the mosque, many

In the bag, the Dream of Flight *is carried to the road from its landing spot outside Peshawar.*

186

of which had powerful public-address systems attached to the highest minarets. Each village also had its bazaar, a row of rectangular, frontless shops, a bit like boxcars on a train.

By the time we stopped near Bahawalpur in the early afternoon my face was black with dust and the corpses of countless mosquitoes and other creatures of possible entomological interest. We went to a rest house to wash and then to a room where our lunch was set out on what appeared to be a tablecloth with a floral design. On closer examination, it turned out that the cloth was only plain white linen on which deli-

There's a stretch of road from Multan to Lahore that transverses a great swamp. When the rains come, the road is swallowed up, leaving only a narrow muddy track.

Bicycle rickshaws escort the Team into Lodhran, a town of about 10,000.

cate flower petals had been meticulously arranged.

We moved out immediately following the meal, and within just a few minutes came to Lodhran, a town of about ten thousand, where we were asked to make an unscheduled stop. It seemed the villagers did not want our arrival to go uncelebrated. Garlands of fragrant wild roses were draped over our heads, and hot tea and cold soda were served. It was a pleasant and quite unexpected show of hospitality, and we appreciated it. Still, we had a long way to travel and were eager to get on.

But the festivities in our honor were not over yet. Waiting for us on the road out of town were two long parallel lines of pedal- and moped-powered rickshaws. Behind this cordon were hundreds of waving and cheering villagers.

We crept along on the motorcycles until we were stopped again, this time while a band of bagpipers and drummers performed in the road. Next, a white horse in a pink hat was

introduced to us. It did a remarkable little dance. Then, what appeared to be a group of scantily clad women emerged from the crowd and began to undulate provocatively to the music.

This struck me as extremely peculiar. Is-

Sporting garlands of fragrant wild roses.

lamic law is more than just strict where women and sex are concerned. We had hardly even seen a woman since our arrival in the country. There had been none at any of the receptions, meals or press conferences we had attended so far. Those women we passed while riding had been veiled from head to toe in accord with the dictates of purdah, the Muslim custom of total feminine modesty. Unlike the men and children, women did not generally smile or wave at us. Some even turned their backs until we had passed. When we watched television in our hotel rooms, scenes containing even the most innocent suggestions of sex would routinely be blacked out by the censor. I recall, in particular, the screen going dark just after David Jans-

sen proposed to Gena Rowlands in *Two-Minute Warning.*

Yet here was a group of women boldly flaunting their flesh for our amusement. Only as I inched closer on my motorcycle was I able to discern that, in fact, these seductive dancers were not women at all but rather young boys dressed up as women—traditional entertainers known as khusra dancers, as I was later to be told.

Up ahead, a dancing horse greets Harley horsepower.

As we watched the show, villagers began to filter through the lines of vehicles to ask for an autograph or a shake of the hand. We tried to oblige, of course, but soon there were dozens of hands and pens and pieces of paper flapping like crazed birds in front of our faces. The temperature was pushing into the high nineties, and the sun beat down with relentless intensity. The heat from the idling motors added to the discomfort, while the moist, cloyingly sweet flowers hung like nooses around our necks.

As the crowd pressed closer and more insistently upon us, I found myself becoming dizzy and just a little uneasy. We knew that everyone here meant only to be friendly. But under conditions like these, crowds had been known to transform into mobs, and mobs sometimes lose control. Just when the heat and the pressure of the bodies were beginning to grow unbearable, a contingent of policemen stepped in wielding swagger sticks, forcing the multitude a safe distance away. A path was cleared down the center of the road, and we accelerated rapidly, feeling the relief of the wind in our faces again. The sky grew cloudy and soon a cool rain had begun to fall.

Wherever the Team gassed up, the curious gathered.

By five o'clock we reached the driveway of the Hotel Sinbad in the city of Multan. We had been on the road for 10½ hours, covering only slightly more ground than on Wednesday. Multan is known for its hot, dry climate, said to be the result of a curse cast upon the city by a saint who was flogged to death here centuries ago. But the curse had evidently been lifted for our visit; that evening it rained again as we went for a tour of Multan's ancient forts and domed mausoleums.

The metallic, melodic sound of muezzins calling the faithful to prayer over loudspeakers woke us at five o'clock on Friday morning. The rain had continued throughout the night, and though the sky was now almost cloudless, the streets were still glassy as we rode out of town at dawn. I put on my full-face helmet to protect my skin from the inevitable reappearance of the searing spring sun. April was, after all, the height of the dry season. These unusual rains, everyone kept telling us, couldn't continue.

We drove through the outskirts of the city, passing open stalls dimly illuminated by orange fires. In other shops rows of cola and orange soda bottles glinted like stained glass in the sunshine. The homey smell of bread wafted toward us. On wooden cots strung with hemp, turbaned men reclined, sipping steamy cups of pale tea and smoking hookahs. Others sat in chairs in the shade as barbers tended to their grooming. The beards of the younger men were soot black. The older men often wore bright orange whiskers, turned that color by liberal applications of henna. Veiled women moved in and out of the shadows, shadows themselves, it seemed.

Much has been written about the veil and what it implies regarding the status of women in the Islamic world. But perhaps one might also argue, if not entirely persuasively, that the veil represents an astonishing homage to feminine beauty. The implicit suggestion, after all, is that every woman possesses a physical power so overwhelming that for a man even to gaze upon it could be disastrous. Surely, too, there is something egalitarian in veiling all women, young and old, fat or slender, lovely or hideous. And if nothing else, the custom of purdah means a woman doesn't have to worry about

Time and again the Team heard, "It almost never rains in Pakistan this time of year." (LEFT) Copper-and-brass-ware shops in Peshawar, capital of the Northwest Frontier Province, only a few miles from the border with Russian-occupied Afghanistan. Some 2 million Afghan refugees live in the camps that surround the city.

There is something strangely egalitarian in the custom of purdah.

looking her very best every time she leaves the house.

We rode northeast toward Lahore at a slow but steady clip until eight-thirty, when we came upon a line of several hundred trucks waiting to cross a flood-damaged dirt roadway. Only a single muddy lane was passable, so the trucks had to wait their turn, alternating with trucks coming the other way. With some difficulty, we managed to slowly squeeze by and cross the soggy, rutted road. The minibus and balloon truck were not able to get through so easily, so we had to leave them to catch up later.

It began to drizzle again at about ten o'clock. Then came a brief shower of hail, and after that the rains grew steadily stronger. The road was covered with a thick coating of sickly yellow liquid. Depressions in the road became treacherous bogs. I was riding behind Malcolm, expecting that at any moment he would pull over

Pakistan · 191

On the road to Khyber Pass.

to wait the rain out or to find out if there might not be another route over higher ground. But he continued on undaunted.

Up ahead I saw what appeared to be a swamp covering the road. Malcolm, for some reason, wasn't stopping or even slowing down, as far as I could tell. It occurred to me that he might not be paying attention, but Malcolm isn't that sort of rider. Then, to my amazement and horror, he drove straight into the water. I was almost expecting some variation on the biblical theme. Instead, his wheels half submerged, sending up a long, curving rooster tail of sludge. But he kept on going and came out the other side. Reluctantly, I followed.

Flooded sections of the road began to confront us with increasing frequency. I tried lifting my legs as I went through them, hoping to keep from becoming entirely drenched by the jaundice-colored muck. Soon enough I resigned myself to the fact that no combination of bodily contortions was going to keep me any cleaner or drier. Since the motorcycle I was riding had no windshield, the slop even flowed over my head. At least I had worn my full-face helmet as protection against the sun; without it I would have been eating the stuff as well.

The strain of this kind of riding was wearing on me, but, glancing at the odometer, I knew

we would stop for fuel before long. I could then suggest we break for lunch and a little rest. Even just a short break would have been welcome. But, curiously, Malcolm continued to press on. Before long, I saw Tim switch to his reserve fuel tank and then pull over, out of gas. Malcolm didn't stop. Kip was the next to drop out. Malcolm kept going. As we entered Lahore and caught sight of the real Minar-e-Pakistan in the distance, Jim, too, ran out of gas and pulled over to wait for assistance from our escorts. Malcolm droned on. Finally, only Denny and I, both riding bikes with oversize gas tanks, were able to follow Malcolm—whose bike was equipped with a gas tank of only standard size. At last, I saw Malcolm switch to his reserve tank. Surely now, I thought, he'll stop at a gas station. He couldn't be hoping to make it all the way to the hotel without a stop.

But Malcolm persevered, riding, it seemed to me, more on will than on gasoline. I counted the miles until his reserve tank ran dry. When it did, he pulled the choke. It took me a few minutes to figure out his intention. Remarkable, I thought. He's trying to eke out a little more mileage by riding on fumes. He was. And what's more, it appeared he was going to win this little contest he had set up for himself: The hotel finally came into view. But not quite. There was a divider in the road and the turn-around was another 50 yards farther on. Right there, directly across from the hotel driveway on the wrong side of the divider, Malcolm's bike finally coasted to a halt.

Within a few seconds two policemen arrived. They gripped the motorcycle from behind and, with Malcolm still sitting tall in the saddle, pushed him to the turnaround and back down the road to the hotel driveway. It was an image I'll not soon forget: Malcolm, aided by his two uniformed assistants, rolling toward the elegant Intercontinental Hotel entrance, a hoodlum maharajah wearing soaking wet leather and a dignified mien.

"So close," Malcolm mumbled as the distressed hotel reception committee shook his dripping hand. "I was there. If it wasn't for that divider I would have made it."

Waking at five on Saturday morning, I looked

out the window to see clear skies and the leaves on the trees motionless—perfect weather for flying balloons. I felt a sense of relief. My guess was that Malcolm's grim display of determination on the way to Lahore yesterday stemmed, at least in part, from our inability to raise the *Minar* in Karachi and concern that we would not be able to raise it anywhere else.

Local newspapers had written of our "failure," and polite but vaguely condescending officials had been telling us how sorry they had been to hear that we "were not very success-ful." One thing seemed certain: This trip, which had already become something of an endurance test, was likely to become a lot more trying if the weather did not clear and the *Minar* did not rise pretty soon.

We drove by bus to the Qaddafi Stadium, named for the mercurial Libyan leader, where a crowd of several thousand had already begun to gather. "Well, if the *Minar* doesn't get up here, we can blame it on Qaddafi," Malcolm quipped. We all chuckled, a little tensely.

The balloon was laid out as it had been in

The crowd in Lahore applauds the successful inflation of the Minar.

The Minar *stretched out in Qaddafi Stadium, Lahore.*

Karachi, and the fans were switched on. The weather still seemed to be all right, but the central problem remained: how to get the hot air to the far end of the balloon, 230 feet away from the source of heat. Denny had an idea. He and Malcolm took a propane tank and a burner and walked directly into the interior of the balloon. They came back out as far toward the end as they could and cooked the air there, then slowly backtracked, spraying fire as they went. Malcolm climbed into the gondola for the final blasts of heat.

The balloon rose slightly, still parallel to the ground. It wriggled awkwardly as it tried to rise, but it appeared that it was not yet able to do so. As Malcolm manned the burner, fire sprinkled over the balloon's nylon skirt, making Swiss cheese of it.

But slowly, very slowly, the *Minar* was beginning to ascend. Again, that awkward bend appeared in the center, making the balloon look more like a sloppily handled tube of toothpaste than a national monument. Then, within no more than two or three seconds, the balloon majestically straightened and floated skyward. Applause exploded from the audience as the balloon rose higher, taking the gondola, with Malcolm in it, off the ground. In triumph, he waved to the crowd. A feeble breeze began to blow, and the *Minar*, now straight and tall, inclined like the Leaning Tower of Pisa. Still, it was working—the world's tallest balloon was flying—and Malcolm was suspended exuberantly beneath it.

The Minar *is saluted by the army band.*

At 240 feet, the Minar *is the tallest balloon in the world.*

194 · Around the World on Hot Air & Two Wheels

FORBES MAGAZINE
HAILS
PAKISTAN-U.S.
FRIENDSHIP

فوربز میگزین
پاک امریکہ دوستی کو سلام کرتا ہے

With uncharacteristic prudence, he decided not to untie the tethers. Instead he quickly came back down to earth, then erected the *Dream of Flight* and took off with Denny and a shaky Pakistani television cameraman for a brief free flight in that.

"Our effort to salute Pakistan was successful," a much relieved Malcolm later told a radio interviewer. "The *Minar* has been raised in its home city."

By noon a much more relaxed motorcycle gang was on the road once more, traveling northwest toward the twin cities of Rawalpindi and Islamabad. Though pewter clouds appeared in the distant sky, for the most part they held their moisture. The land was becoming more fertile, and the geography began to grow more interesting, the road twisting through a corrugated landscape of green and brown hills. When we reached Rawalpindi toward late afternoon, the odometer on my motorcycle indicated that we had covered a distance of 975 miles since our journey began on the previous Tuesday.

We rose at five on Sunday and, over breakfast, read about ourselves in the *Pakistan Times*. The article reported that the *Minar* had been inflated and that the *Dream of Flight* had flown. "Mr. Forbes felt elated at the success of both ventures after his failures in Karachi and said he was glad not to have disappointed the people of Lahore," the article concluded.

But not content to let us rest on his laurels, Malcolm planned to fly the balloons again today, so by six forty-five we were off for the Rawalpindi race course.

Denny used the same method to inflate the

Army recruits help unpack the Minar.

Despite the failure to get the Minar *aloft in Karachi, the crowd greeted the Team with tremendous warmth.*

Minar as he had in Lahore. In addition, extra nitrogen was added to the propane in the gondola's tank in an attempt to project the flames still deeper into the balloon. But when the *Minar* was inflated and Malcolm hit the trigger, the nitrogen-rich mixture ignited explosively, spitting a wide arc of fire across the already

Watching the Dream of Flight *take off from the Peshawar stadium.*

perforated skirt of the balloon. Under such intense heat, the material began simply to melt away. To make matters worse, after the balloon began to rise, the locally hired crew didn't hear the signal to release the ropes holding down the far end. As a consequence, the *Minar* jackknifed again, and only after several suspenseful minutes did it manage to unfold.

Malcolm rose briefly into the air, acknowledged the applause of the crowd, then set down and ordered the *Minar* deflated. Clouds filled the sky, and the rain began to fall once more. The crowd scattered while we hastily packed up and returned to the hotel.

We left Rawalpindi at one-thirty, passing through mostly barren landscape, crossing the silty Indus River and entering the North West Frontier Province early in the afternoon. Along the roadsides and by the riverbanks we began to see the squalid camps of the Afghan refugees. Bearded men with disheveled turbans piled atop their heads squatted in the dust in front of tents stamped with UNHCR (for United Nations High Commissioner for Refugees) while veiled women tended black iron pots suspended over smoky fires. "Soviets Out of Afghanistan" I saw scrawled across a plastered wall.

More than 3 million refugees have now crossed the border from Afghanistan into Paki-

Young friends on the road to Abbottabad.

The Dream of Flight, *decorated with the mythological figures of flight, takes off in Peshawar.*

stan. Some are guerrillas who remain only long enough to rest, recuperate and attempt to obtain additional arms and ammunition. Many others have no plans to return to their ravaged homeland. Because of close ethnic and linguistic links with the local population, the refugees

The traffic backed up for miles when the road disappeared into a muddy track south of Lahore.

Floating toward Afghanistan.

The countryside around Peshawar as it looks from a balloon basket.

tend to find easy acceptance in the region. But the sheer weight of their numbers has put tremendous pressure on meager water resources and sharply increased competition for scarce employment.

Late in the afternoon, as a light rain was falling, we reached our hotel in the 2,000-year-old city of Peshawar, capital of the North West Frontier Province, and centuries ago an important stop on the great trade routes from Persia, China and Turkistan.

Early Monday morning we set off for the Peshawar Stadium. Yet another "balloon demonstration" was on the schedule. Malcolm explained to the crowd that the *Minar* would not be inflated, however; it would be returning to England for repairs and modifications. Then, with Denny and an English newspaper photographer accompanying him in the *Dream of Flight*, Malcolm took off for a long flight over the quiet countryside.

As afternoon approached we left Peshawar for the Khyber Pass leading to Afghanistan, a rugged road between the mountains where more than a century ago the soldiers of Victorian Britain waged bloody battles against fierce Pathan warriors whose way of life remains largely unchanged even today. The Khyber Pass lies in what is known as the tribal belt, a region still ruled by local chiefs free of effective

An old man gets a new story to tell his grandchildren.

Pakistan · 199

government control. The tribal belt remains as wild and unconquered as any corner of the earth today. And for most of the past six months, two of the local Pathan tribes had been warring, reportedly over control of the opium trade. Under such conditions, we were told, travel in the area could be hazardous.

Not far outside Peshawar, a pickup truck containing eight Pakistani soldiers armed with automatic rifles and another manning an MG 42 machine gun joined our caravan. This military escort accompanied us to the town of Jamrud, a lone government outpost within the tribal area and the last town before the Bab-e-Khyber, the Gate to the Khyber Pass. As we stopped for fuel a crowd of men gathered. Most wore large turbans and coarse blankets and had rifles slung casually over their shoulders; in the tribal territory almost every male is armed at all times.

Entering Jamrud, a frontier town reminiscent of America's Old West—virtually every male inhabitant is armed at all times.

The leader, menacingly wielding what Jim later identified as a Chinese-made version of an AK-47, shouted at Malcolm in a language that was probably Pushtu. The other two men, both carrying Enfield .303 carbines and wearing bandoliers, watched from the flatbed of the truck.

Turned back in the Khyber Pass by automatic-rifle-toting members of the local constabulary.

We proceeded to the gate and waited for our escorts to take the lead. But they were nowhere to be seen. Malcolm decided to proceed without them. We began our descent down the winding road. We had traveled no more than two or three miles when a Suzuki pickup containing three armed men came charging up from behind. It swerved in front of Malcolm and forced him to a halt.

Passing through the Bab-el-Khyber, the Gate to the Khyber Pass, at Jamrud.

The leader's words may have been incomprehensible, but his meaning was not difficult to divine: We were not supposed to have passed the gate, and we were to turn back immediately. Malcolm didn't argue for a moment. Though not a man who takes no for an answer easily, Malcolm's experiences in World War II and New York City have evidently impressed upon him the virtue of showing courtesy to strangers bearing automatic weapons. Later, we were to learn that these persuasive gentlemen were informal representatives of the local constabulary. A journey through the pass could not be risked at this time, it had been decided; our demise might tarnish the image of the neighborhood.

I was still thinking about these events later that afternoon when the death occurred. As happens not infrequently when riding a motorcycle in the countryside, a bird flew into my path, its white wings flapping wildly in the air ahead. (I was reminded of the birdlike profusion of papers that had waved in my face in Lodhran earlier.) I slowed sharply to give it time to maneuver out of my way as birds normally manage to do. But for some reason the animal panicked and headed directly for me. Before I could react, I saw the beak pointing toward my eye. Luckily for me, the visor on my helmet was down. The bird's luck, however, had run out. My head snapped back as it hit with a heavy smack. Blood splattered across my helmet. "You got him," said Denny, driving up from behind.

Just minutes later, Malcolm found himself in a far more frightening situation. As he came around a turn, a small child darted into the road in front of him. Malcolm slammed his brakes and went into a skid, barely missing the child and narrowly avoiding a spill as his back wheel slid out to the right.

We reached the town of Abbottabad, in the foothills of the Himalayas, by five o'clock. A precipitous road took us to a mountaintop rest house, a lovely colonial cottage with a view of the snow-capped mountains. As darkness fell, a low, solemn drone rose from the dwellings scattered in the valley below, a mournful, discordant dirge, the sound of faithful Muslims raising their voices in prayer.

Villagers scratch out an existence from the terraces cut in rocky mountainsides along the Karakorum Highway.

A spectacular, primeval valley high in the Karakorums.

The rains began again early Tuesday morning. The newspapers called them "torrential" and reported that a more rainy April in Pakistan could not be recalled. One consequence was that mud and rock slides had begun to occur along the mountain road to our north. With unusual prudence, Malcolm decided that we would go no further by motorcycle.

Instead, we proceeded by car, accompanied by Brigadier Jan Nadir Khan, the intelligent and dignified president of the Adventure Foundation. The route took us to the first stretches of the famous Karakorum Highway (KKH), the two-lane road that connects Pakistan with China, along an agonizingly twisting route through four of the world's great mountain ranges: the Karakorums, the Himalayas, the Hindu Kush and the Pamir. The KKH, which was completed only in 1979, took twenty years to build. Thousands of Pakistanis and Chinese took part in the mammoth construction. Hundreds of them were killed in landslides and accidents before the project was finished.

We returned to Abbottabad in the late afternoon and immediately packed up to begin the

As the sign suggests, landslides are common along the Karakorum Highway. Below: The highway, connecting China and Pakistan, twists up the Indus and Gilgit river gorges through four of the world's great mountain ranges.

final ride back to Rawalpindi. The rain was coming down harder, and the road looked slippery. I was particularly nervous about the journey since the motorcycle I had been riding had no windshield or crashbar and the headlight and horn had both ceased working long ago.

As we left Abbottabad I saw a billboard that seemed to articulate my fears. It read: "Life Is Uncertain." (The tag line went: "Life Insurance Is Certain.")

Any chance of getting back to Rawalpindi before dark was lost around six o'clock when Malcolm's bike rolled to a halt. It turned out that a line from the gas tank had come loose and his fuel had spilled onto the road. Denny took a small piece of wire and managed to use it to reattach the line. Malcolm then switched to his reserve fuel tank and we were able to continue.

As darkness fell, Jim "cradled" me, as he put it, running interference for me against the oncoming traffic while I stayed behind him and as close as possible to the road's edge. I couldn't see much through my rain-washed visor. I simply followed the red taillight on Jim's bike and that on Malcolm's further ahead. When the red lights became bigger, I slowed down; when they became smaller, I sped up. When they jumped, I prepared for a bump. I felt as if I were playing

some video arcade game rather than riding a motorcycle. Every so often I had to raise my visor to allow the cool, wet air to break the hypnotic spell.

Finally, around seven-thirty we rolled into the safety of the hotel driveway in Rawalpindi. According to my odometer we had covered nearly thirteen hundred miles of rainy road since first firing up the engines in Karachi a week before.

We did not ride the motorcycles or launch the balloons again in Pakistan. On Wednesday we dressed in coats and ties and went by minibus to nearby Islamabad for a reception with General Zia. Malcolm presented him with one of our motorcycle vests, which he gamely donned. The general, in turn, awarded Malcolm Pakistan's "Pride of Performance" medal. "The honors you least deserve, you most appreciate," Malcolm noted.

Malcolm also promised, in addition to repairing and modifying the Minar balloon, to build a conventionally shaped balloon for Pakistan, one that could be used in competition. And he reiterated his pledge to bring a team of athletes from the Adventure Foundation to the United

MSF is awarded the "Pride of Performance" medal by General Zia, President of Pakistan, before 200 assembled government officials and legislators.

States to be trained in its operation and maintenance.

We were not at all pleased that the expedition was coming to an end. Our time in Pakistan seemed to have passed with blistering speed. We had been on the move every day, crossing more than three-quarters of the length of the country. But there remained much we hadn't seen as well, including most of the dramatic northern region, where Pakistan boasts eight of the world's ten tallest mountains. And we knew only too well that we had barely glimpsed a few of the highlights of the many regions through which we had traveled.

If the weather had been less than cooperative, our Pakistani hosts had more than compensated for it. If the riding had been difficult, with far too many mishaps and close calls for comfort, as seasoned motorcyclists we knew better than to complain about any trip we could walk away from. The world's tallest balloon may not have turned out to be the world's best balloon, but at least it reached the sky as it was intended to do.

Most important for us, perhaps, Pakistan from now on would no longer be just current events and a list of Kiplingesque names on the map. Khyber, Peshawar, the Punjab, the Sind, these places meant something to us now. As the world's only international goodwill motorcycle gang, we hoped we had managed to bring a message of good wishes and good intentions to the thousands upon thousands of Pakistanis we had greeted. Certainly, that was the message they had given us to take back home.

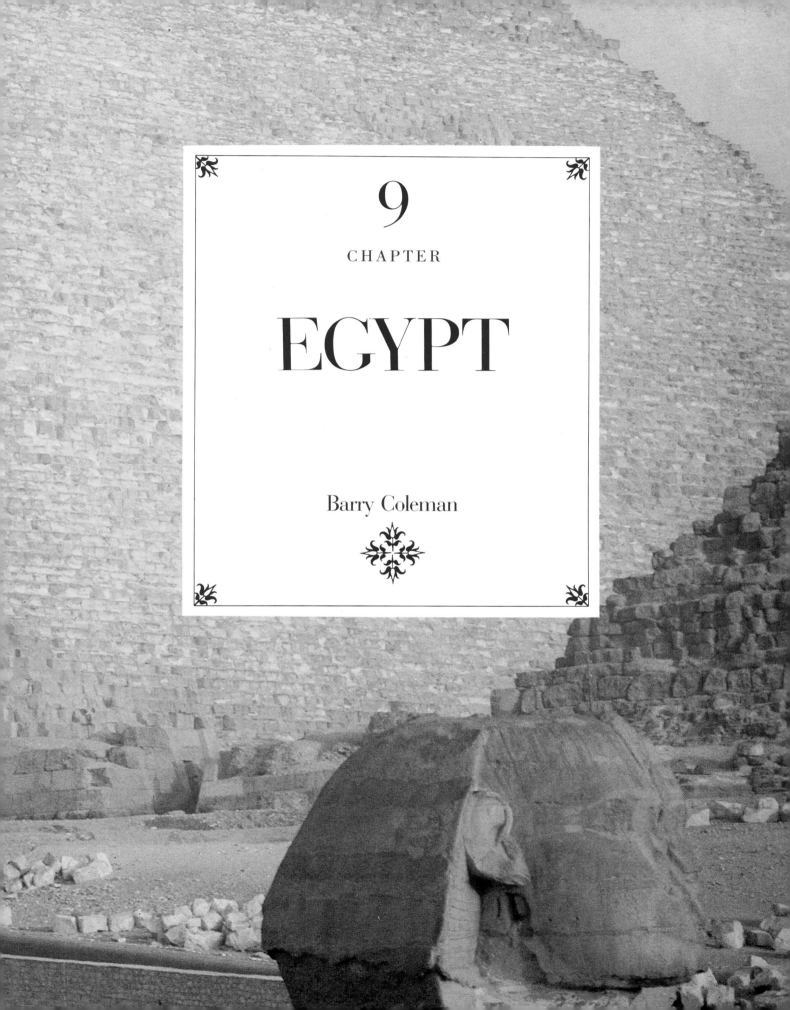

9

CHAPTER

EGYPT

Barry Coleman

MEMO TO THE WHITE HOUSE
STATUS: *Restricted*

Listen, Joey, before I start this report, I think I should recommend that you keep a pretty tight rein on who sees it. It could be dynamite. I mean to say, a friend of the President takes it into his head to conduct unofficial diplomatic missions to touchy places all over the world, spreading American goodwill. That's one thing. I guess goodwill comes under the heading of free enterprise, and we can live with it. But that's not the point. It's the way he does it.

You may recall when we first heard about it, you said, well, what's the problem, just a friendly old guy, all American, out to say hi to the natives and you signed a requisition for a standard-issue bulletproof vest and a darkened limousine, extra long, to take his buddies in? Well let me tell you, Joey, it didn't quite work out that way. I went along, like you said I should, posing as a writer for some dumb magazine, and one way or another, all hell was let loose. No problem, you say? Not for you, maybe. But I have to tell you that this guy conducts his diplomacy from the little wicker compartment that hangs below a hot-air balloon. And let me tell you how else he gets around these countries. Get ready for this, Joey, because you're not going to like it: He rides a motorcycle.

I have to confess that we saw it coming. We even tried to keep it from you while we tried to

Sinai, where Moses, understandably, got completely lost.

FORBES MAGAZINE HAILS
EGYPTIAN - U.S. AMITY

Aloft at the Pyramids.

Sometimes even we don't believe what we're seeing.

talk him out of it. But I'm afraid that's it, Joey: balloons and motorcycles. Not only that, but this amiable gray-haired buddy of the chief, this unofficial diplomatist who, at the outside, is supposed to be glad-handing bigwigs behind the well-closed doors of the private dining rooms of the grandest hotels, is out leading a flag-waving procession of motorcycles round the Pyramids, up the Nile, through the desert, you name it, with sirens wailing and Harley-Davidsons thundering like some sort of scarlet and chrome earthquake.

I know what you're thinking, Joey. But really, there was nothing I could do to stop it. I think you're going to have to take a look at the file. You see, it has a lot to do with how the whole thing started. He was invited. Really invited. I mean, the thing is, he was invited by Mrs. Mubarak.

I suppose it would have happened at some embassy reception. She would have been intro-

Egypt · 211

duced to this charming full-dress American publisher and said: "Well, Mr. Forbes, your hobbies sound most fascinating. You really must come to see us in Egypt again soon, and perhaps you can even bring one of your balloons, or a motorcycle with you." As innocent as that. But this guy needs no second bidding, as we now know.

I'm sure all this is in the file, but I think you ought to know that he already has a record. He's done this sort of thing before.

First of all, he rode, more or less casually, all the way through Europe to Moscow. No real problem there, and you can't fault it for goodwill. The only slight hint of humorous unreliability came when he presented the mayor with a necktie with the *Forbes* motto "Capitalist

Tool" bannered across it. As we heard it, the mayor's smile was a mite frosty.

Next, though, came the trip to China. It kind of hit the fan there. Both State and the Pentagon have probably got files a foot thick. You can get the details from our own records boys. It should be enough to tell you that the Chinese spent three weeks escorting the Forbes party at 25 mph (which motorcyclists appear to find a little irksome) and telling them they couldn't let their balloon off its tether. Again, to be frank, it was ok on goodwill until for some reason as yet undisclosed, the balloon "accidentally" escaped. Fine, Joey, except that the Chinese had a collective heart attack and the balloon landed smack in the middle of a grade 1-A-restricted military installation.

(BELOW) *Gas stops—unfailing sources of entertainment.*

There's nothing quite so encouraging as a banner that reads "Welcome."

As if that's not enough, this Forbes just happens to run into the president of Pakistan, who says, all wide-eyed, how fascinating, Mr. Forbes, you really must come and see us in Pakistan some time, and maybe you can bring one of your balloons, or even a motorcycle.

There you have it, Joey. A few months later, there's this wild procession of Harley-Davidsons, complete with police escort, thundering from the Arabian Sea to the Himalayas and arriving in Islamabad to a full-scale presidential reception. And here's this balloonist, right there in the presidency, in front of the TV cameras, balloonist, mind you, making droll remarks about the F-16s that are sure to follow. You'd better check that out with you-know-who; make sure they got them. See what I mean?

I got to Cairo a few days before the main party. And what a party. There's Forbes; his two sons, Bob and Tim; three guys from the Forbes HQ in New York, Denny Fleck, Kip Cleland, and Jay Gissen; Norredeine Khadaddi from Forbes in Morocco (they have places all over the world, which doesn't make all this any easier); two journalists from Germany, Dieter

MSF caught, uncharacteristically, waiting.

The Harleys, not exactly desert bikes, did exceptionally well, all things considered.

Vogt and Jurgen Rohrscheid; another from France, Gilles Mermet; a vast number of people seconded by the Egyptian tourism department; some security people, and me.

It would have been fairly easy to hide in the crowd, except that the only magazine I could think of for cover was a motorcycle magazine, and they kept asking me to look after the bikes. Terrific idea, Joey. Have you any idea how often these Harley-Davidsons break down? And how little I know about fixing motorcycles?

Anyhow, by the time we were ready to start the trip in earnest (officially called "the Forbes Festival," by the way), we had acquired considerable local status—TV, newspapers, magazines: all the mechanics of notability.

You know why that was, Joey? Because a party of Americans in black leather riding suits and bright red vests emblazoned with dazzling and symbolic badges had come bearing goodwill? No, I don't think so. Not quite. There were other factors at work here, ones we should take serious note of. For example, this Forbes had come to Egypt with a special balloon. I don't know if you are aware of this, Joey, but they can make these balloons in all sorts of different shapes. I've heard about flying peanuts, airborne lightbulbs, and even an upwardly mobile pair of pants. But what we came up with left those standing (if you see what I mean). We had come to Egypt complete with a flying Sphinx.

Now a flying Sphinx, in Egypt or anywhere else, is not exactly low-profile, however you look at it. On the other hand, I suppose that in a country that consists mainly of desert, you could even fly a Sphinx in relative private. But that's not quite how Malcolm Forbes looks at these things. So when we did find a nice little piece of sand that Forbes considered suitable for the first flight, it was the piece next to the Pyramids.

That was when I realized what kind of trouble we were in, Joey. I mean the Pyramids are not some hole-in-the-corner tourist way station. The Pyramids are one of mankind's most concentrated gestures of defiance, a flight of geometry whose motivation we can barely glimpse no matter how long we stare at them. They may well have a hole in the corner, but even that took centuries to find. Believe me, Joey, the Pyramids take a lot of beating for profile.

So here we are, riding our Harleys around the Pyramids, in line astern, headlights blazing, and down there by the Sphinx waits the official welcoming party: the governor of Giza (which is where the Pyramids are, local-government-wise), the deputy minister of tourism, officials by the dozen, esteemed guests, and dancing horses. We shimmer down the hill, rumble to a halt, Forbes says hi to the folks, makes a pleasant speech, and suddenly jumps over a little wall and disappears into the desert. Well, we all jump over, and there up ahead is this enormous yellow nylon bag. Turns out to be the *Sphinx.*

You might say it caught the eye. The Sphinx and the *Flying Sphinx* of Forbes and party. It

While the horse danced, the guest of honor jumped over the wall.

Put the Sphinx *over there, next to the Sphinx.*

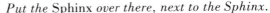

MEDITERRANEAN
SEA

N

Alexandria

Tanta

Giza

Suez
Canal

Ismailia

Cairo

Suez

St. Catherine
Monastery

Nuweiba

El-Minia

Dahab

Asyut

Nile River

Sharm
El-Sheik

SAUDI ARABIA

ISRAEL

Hurghada

RED
SEA

Luxor

Aswan

EGYPT
February 23–
March 14, 1984

● BALLOONING

0 Mi   50   100

0 Km   50   100

As the Old gazes placidly, the New is filled with hot air.

Another dawn at the Pyramids, but this was a dawn with a difference.

So what is it this time?

seems also to have caught the network news in every country you care to name and I notice it was practically a centerfold in *Newsweek*. You have to understand, Joey. There was nothing I could do to stop it. As a matter of fact, it's very hard to stop this guy doing things.

There's more to Egypt than Sphinxes, Joey. The day after the first flight we set off for Alexandria. Wonderful name, terrific reputation in

A bit more traditional than riding a flying Sphinx.

history, literature and myth, but on the face of it, truth to tell, not much of a place. We flew the balloon in a soccer stadium, which was full of politely appreciative people, but I had a slightly chill feeling for a moment there. Maybe Alexandria, cosmopolitan jewel of the Mediterranean with a history so colorful you need dark glasses just to think about it had already seen all it needed by way of goodwill gestures.

Something else crossed my mind. Alexandria is a city of mixed Muslim and Christian communities, and on a nice still night it could probably hear the New Jersey's interesting impression of the battle of Jutland, and as a city it may have been a touch indecisive about how to react to any buddy of the boss, Sphinx or no Sphinx. All this stuff is important on a goodwill mission, Joey. It's the very stuff of which memos are made. And not just ours.

The next day we rode directly away from the sea. I was still anxious, but I have to tell you I was beginning to enjoy the motorcycling. Pretty pleasant, Joey: nice and warm, the Harleys rumbling, the palms nodding in the Delta breeze. Nothing wrong with that.

We stopped for lunch in a town called Tanta. The thing about these Forbes goodwill trips is that you never know quite where you are. You look at the map, but that tells you nothing very much. Everything is arranged by someone else, in this case by a political science teacher who also works at the UN and who also happens to be an Egyptian, name of Yassin el-Ayouti.

The funny thing is though, I learned a lot about goodwill that lunchtime. We found ourselves in a sort of school. We were guided to our seats in a large hall, where presentations were made, with speeches, and a nice little school band played some pretty Arab music. It was just like a visit by the queen of England, except that the royal party were wearing dusty boots, leather suits, and bright red denim vests.

After lunch we went outside, and there we were treated to various displays. Marching

Even the desert gets misty sometimes.

New life, and not a bad one, for the pantomime horse.

220 · Around the World on Hot Air & Two Wheels

Volleyball in Tanta;
no self-pity here.

Malcolm's Ping-Pong wasn't
nearly good enough.

bands, for example, and model airplane flying. The marching wasn't too polished and the plane crashed. But that didn't matter. In fact I began to detect, for the first time since the whole crazy thing started, a kind of warmth.

I couldn't understand it at first, but later on, when I was riding through the desert with a little concentration to spare, it hit me. All these people, like people everywhere, have passions. The passions may be a bit odd, eccentric maybe, and hard to explain to others. But when this Forbes rolls up on his motorcycle, and starts flying wild-looking balloons, they know right off the bat that he's as crazy as they are. No need for words. The passions say it all. I'm not kidding, Joey, this beats all the regular hands-across-the-sea stuff, which, if I may say so, is hardly surprising. We're going to have to take another look at this. Does the chief ride a motorcycle?

Before we left the school, which was also a community development center, we watched some seriously disabled people play pretty good volleyball. No pity there, Joey, no fatal embarrassment about our own good fortune. Just this surprising warmth: motorcycles were our thing, volleyball was theirs. Oh, and Ping-Pong. A guy with no arms beat Malcolm at Ping-Pong and beat him good. Check out the chief's Ping-Pong, will you Joey?

Egypt · 221

After that, it was all ok. We knew what we were there for. That and the adventure. See, all sorts of people go to Egypt, but nobody rides motorcycles up the valley of the Nile. The day after Tanta, we began riding through this untoured territory. And then some really surprising things started happening.

We're riding along on a road that is slightly raised up above the field that the Nile has somehow coaxed out of the desert. We're waving to the folks, and the folks are waving back, from way out there among the crops. As we're riding, we notice that the road is punctuated by fellas standing in the middle of nowhere with rifles slung over their shoulders. For some reason we naturally interpret this, though we don't understand it in the slightest, as a gesture of welcome.

Suddenly up ahead we see a town. And outside the town we can see a kind of multicolored bubbling, which turns out to be the population. As we ride up, four athletes appear, each one holding a corner of the municipal flag. They ran in front of us in the midday heat for at least five miles, every inch of which was shaped into something like a tunnel by the people pressing to get a look, slap a back and shake a hand.

At Aswan the festival turned around and headed back north.

A simple message in English and Arabic.

Coffee stop on the way to Minya.

Turns out there's no welcome like an Egyptian welcome.

Egypt · 223

Every town we came to that day was the same, only each one got more effusive, more frantic. The tunnel got narrower, the goodwill more pressing. I don't know if you know anything about these Harley-Davidsons, Joey. Basically, they're big. They also get hot. And they're awful tricky to ride if you're slipping the clutch with one hand, keeping the throttle barely open with the other, and balancing as well while wildly glad-handing with both of them.

Eventually, two of the inevitables happened. Someone fell off in the melee, and someone found himself riding to a halt through a cloud of thickening black smoke. Terrific for goodwill, however. To the cheers of those lining the roofs as well as the roadside, the fallen Norredeine (who at least could say thanks in Arabic) was hauled upright and the gummed-up Harley was flipped by a cast of hundreds into the back of the El-Minya governorate fire truck, 1923 vintage. If there's one thing that brings strangers together faster than a motorcycle cutting the engineering mustard, it's a motorcycle in dis-

A first for any Harley-Davidson. Welcome aboard the El-Minya fire truck.

tress. I know, because I mended that one later by the curbside in El-Minya city ("No problem —the guy from the motorcycle magazine will fix it") and I knew most of the downtown crowd intimately before I had the air cleaner off.

We spent the next night in a place called Asyut, where we also flew the balloon. Just in case you didn't quite catch the point about how tourists travel in Egypt, let me give you a couple of statistics about Asyut. Number of people: two million. Number of hotels: nil. We stayed in the Physicians Rest House. Let me tell you something else about Egypt. The physicians are tough guys.

Speaking of which, we had an interesting moment in the great center of ancient civilization and modern tourism, Luxor. (You get there by plane and drift back down the Nile to Cairo in a cruiser.)

Up until then, we had flown the *Sphinx* on a tether, which was fine but not quite the real thing. We planned to fly it free in Luxor. The bureaucrats who were along with us had counter-notions. I don't really know why. They just weren't going for it. I guess they felt that free flight implied some more dangerous ideas of freedom and anything might happen. But you

The temple at Luxor; staggering, but a mere curtain-raiser for Karnak, two miles away. (BELOW) Palms against still water: Egypt's supreme version of tranquillity.

In some parts of Egypt, there is simply no substitute for a camel.

Egypt · 225

know the old bureaucrat's code, Joey. If anything was going to be on a line, it was that balloon and not their ass.

Malcolm was great. I loved it. He said ok, but I'll tell you this: One way or another, we'll be flying tomorrow; it may not be in that balloon, but do you want to be the one to explain to Mrs. Mubarak why we're back in New York? There were no takers, and we flew next morning.

We flew again in Aswan a day or so later. Pretty damn spectacular, Joey. As the *Sphinx* drifted out of the town, streams of children flowed out behind it. It was the same every time it flew and more so when it landed. The kids jumped and bounced and giggled all over it. And in the middle of all that you would see Malcolm's grin as big as any of theirs perched like the Cheshire cat's between a bright red shirt and a New York Yacht Club hat.

When we got to the Aswan High Dam (about the builders of which the least said soonest mended, Joey, if you catch my drift), we turned around and started vaguely back toward where we had started from. Just how vague it was at times we'll come to in a minute. Meanwhile I ought maybe to give a little of the slightly more formal background to all this, if formal's the word.

A Sphinx-*eye view of the launching party, in Aswan.* (RIGHT) *The* Sphinx *over Aswan—a little surprising, even for the initiated.*

The Pied Piper effect beginning to develop in the streets of Aswan.

The kids couldn't get enough of the Sphinx—literally.

Every night, all the way up the Nile, to the very point where the crocodiles begin (they can't get through the dam, so the paddlers of Cairo have at least that to thank the Soviets for), we were the guests at official receptions held by governors, mayors, and other bigwigs. It's hard to grasp, isn't it? You ride all day—

Egypt · 227

six, seven, eight hours—you arrive in time to fly the world's most complicated balloon for a stadiumful of cheering citizenry. That done, you hurtle back to the hotel, fling your leather jacket in a corner, grab a white shirt (slightly crumpled), wrestle for your life with a Forbes Magazine Balloon Ascension Division tie, throw on a dark-blue blazer, gray pants and a nicely polished pair of shoes, and fly back out again to shake hands with the governor and knock back a handful of the local kebabs.

Now it turns out that the man Forbes is pretty good at engaging and charming the local authorities. He pins nice enamel Sphinx campaign medals on them for a start, and he makes good jokes. There's no doubt it puts a new light on Americans for these guys. Now they know we wear crumpled shirts.

I suppose I should also mention that we took in the antiquities in passing. The Valley of the Kings, for example. We dived into the tombs of King Tut (who, as you know, gave his life for tourism) and a whole bunch of the Rameses boys. Those tombs are breathtaking for their scale, their artistic detail, and the assumption of wholesale reincarnation that underlies them.

Every tomb tells a story of astonishing complexity.

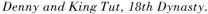
Denny and King Tut, 18th Dynasty.

Tut-Ankh-Amun was too young to build up much of
a picture; but when it comes to immortality, he got
the last laugh.

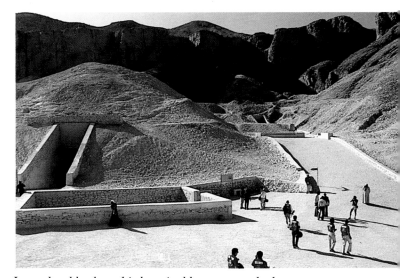

In such a bleak and inhospitable graveyard, the wonder is that the kings were ever found.

Egypt · 229

The map's markings must have shown "secondary road."

230 · Around the World on Hot Air & Two Wheels

Malcolm passed over this point one evening at a reception. "Your cultural heritage is unique and marvelous, something at which the whole world stands in wonder. But I don't know. I mean, as far as I can see, dead is dead." I must say I thought he had finally dropped the diplomatic ball right there, but the dignitaries thought it was a hoot. I don't know, Joey. I have a feeling that if you ride a motorcycle to the party and bring your own balloon, Sphinxlike or otherwise, you can get away with anything.

We left the Nile at a place called Kena and headed toward the Red Sea. This is where I sort of felt the motorcycling really began, although we'd already done a thousand miles of pretty good stuff.

You know all about the influence of the Nile on the Egyptian economy, culture, lifestyle and everything else, but what you may not know is just how precisely that influence can be measured. About a mile out of Kena, a couple of miles from the river, green Egypt stopped, and yellow Egypt began. It doesn't fade gradually. On one side of a wall, or maybe a ditch, is the lushest, most verdant, most productive green. On the other side is the most aseptically barren desert you will ever see. A cactus, let alone manna, would be a miracle.

The Forbes Festival looked terrific rolling through the desert. Out front was the security vehicle, blue light flashing seriously onward through the sandy void. Then the Harleys: an FXRT, three FXRSs, a Sturgis, a Soft-tail, and a Low Rider, which seems to be another name for a red Sturgis. Behind the Harleys came the three mini-buses with the officials, the luggage, the journalists, and the film crew. Then the assorted emergency, police and unattributed vehicles that joined in, followed by two gigantic orange trucks crashing along in the rear with all the ballooning stuff scrambled up inside. I mention this now because a half-hour later two of the FXRSs checked out. Of course, they had been to China and Pakistan, so they were forgiven. Later the guy from the motorcycle magazine raised one of them from the dead, using donor parts from the other. If I were H-D, I'd call my next model the Phoenix.

On our second day in the desert we ran out

In peace, the Suez tunnel dips straight under the Bar-Lev line.

An honor conferred: Sheikh Malcolm of Dahab.

Signposts have taken the place of gun emplacements.

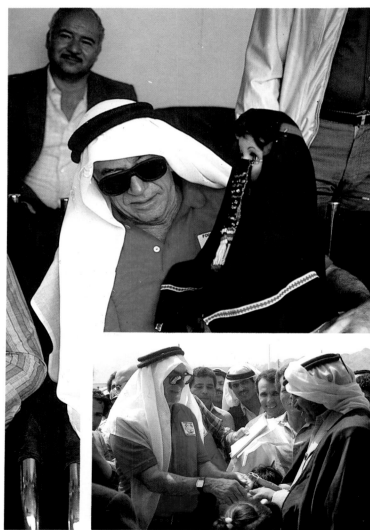

of road. The asphalt took us a hundred miles or so up the coast and then stopped. A rock-strewn track, axle-deep in soft red sand, meandered on from there. We rode at it pretty manfully because we had no choice, but we would rather have sat on a rock complaining about the map, which showed it as an "international highway." You don't ride sideways with your rear wheel spinning down most international highways, but worse than that was that it showed some of the roads we were due to ride as "tracks." When we finally got out on something resembling hard top, maybe fifty miles south of Suez, we saw a notice saying not to forget that this was the road that Moses used. Well, poor Moses. But at least he wasn't riding a full-dress FXRT.

When we rode through the new tunnel that goes at a stroke under the Suez canal and the Bar-Lev line, we were reminded of all-too-recent history. We had gotten so used to the

The Bedouin elders of Suez: if they were baffled, they surely didn't show it. (BELOW) Camel enthusiasts, professional . . . and amateur.

friendliness of the Egyptians and their amazing capacity for putting on a welcome that we had almost forgotten the hostilities, let alone the fact that we had been pretty consistently on the other side. But that's the thing about hostilities, don't you find? Sometimes it's harder than hell to remember just what they were all about. Not that that seems to make them any easier to avoid. The desert on the Sinai side was littered with dead tanks, whose vulnerability turned out to have outweighed their other qualities. From that distance you couldn't see whose they were. And oddly enough, it doesn't seem to matter.

We visited some holiday villages on the Gulf of Aqaba built by the Israelis and largely stranded by Camp David. They were close to Eilat, to Israel, but somehow they seem an awful long way from anywhere else. Business there is not brisk, and I think someone should do a memo about it. Not least because the Sinai desert is without question one of the most beautiful places on God's Earth.

The Sinai welcoming committee.

Ballooning had never made so many conquests all at once.

234 · Around the World on Hot Air & Two Wheels

Greetings from the middle of nowhere.

Suez, a battered and beleaguered town, takes offers of friendship seriously—with both hands.

When you go to St. Catherine's, take the long way round.

It was when we left the Gulf of Aqaba coast that we ran into what the map (with typical overstatement) described as "track." Depends on your idea of track, I suppose. When we started out, you could just make out the track from the desert on either side. But that was before the sandstorm. What we got was blinded and pretty well bowled over by one of the worst blows in those parts for years.

Don't let anyone tell you all Harley-Davidsons can do is cruise idly down some turnpike at half the legal limit. These things are dynamite in the rough stuff, Joey. Unstoppable. A little cumbersome to be sure unless you keep on the gas, but money in the bank if you're ready to close your eyes, wind her open and put all your trust in Milwaukee.

There's just one thing. The luggage. Panniers and top boxes don't seem to sit too well in the desert air. The FXRT just wasn't going for it, and after about a couple of hours, I saw both it and Malcolm fly upwards and outwards, arms, legs, wheels, tanks, panniers, helmet and ass, not necessarily in that order, going everywhere. It wasn't a perfect moment, Joey, as you can imagine. Here's the boss's buddy circulating somewhere above the Sinai desert, miles if not days from the nearest doctor, let alone hospital, in company with half a ton of highly mobile and very spiky-looking steel. Not looking, at that particular point, like the stuff of which happy memos are made.

It was all a bit of a blur in the sand, but when we got to him, he was lying underneath the world's heaviest motorcycle and not moving so much as a millimeter in any direction. We dragged the bike off and after a second or two, as if inspired by some sudden thought, he jumped up. We put him in the van for an hour or so, by which time we had reached the spectacular haven of Saint Catherine's monastery.

Saint Catherine's is a relatively secluded residence at the foot of Mount Sinai, where Moses received one of the biggest briefings of all time. Pilgrims have gone there since at least the fifth century, and still do, though now by coach from Cairo or Jerusalem. My guess is that they take the long way round.

Mount Sinai, scene of a brief, but memorable, encounter.

"On the beach at Nuweiba."

The Egypt lineup. From the left: Yassın el-Ayouti, Tim Forbes, Barry Coleman, Norredeine Khaddady, *MSF, Jay Gissen, Bob Forbes; (kneeling) Kip Cleland, Denny Fleck.*

The world's biggest wind sock, at Sharm el-Sheikh. *(BELOW)* The new Sphinx *rising, at Luxor, before takeoff.*

FORBES MAGAZINE HAILS
EGYPTIAN-U.S. AMITY

Egypt · 239

We rode back into Cairo in convoy, blue light up front, orange truck somewhere at the back, smashing around in the traffic. Malcolm rode into town at the head of the Harleys, 300 desert miles and a broken rib under his belt that day.

We got to the hotel and he sent out for an order of pain killers. He also sent out orders for a no-quarter diplomatic attempt to get permission to fly the *Sphinx* over Cairo in one final spectacular, never-to-be-forgotten gesture of Forbesism.

Well, I saw it, Joey. I saw the *Sphinx* fly over Cairo. And just before it took off, with Forbes

From the basket of a balloon, a timely reminder.

himself on the burners, I realized why he had jumped up so promptly that day in the sandstorm. There were officials in those vans, Joey, people like us, and he knew that they wouldn't allow a friend of the president's to fly any *Sphinx* over any capital city of theirs with a broken rib. And it wouldn't be his ribs they would be thinking about, Joey. It would be some other part of their own anatomy.

The Sphinx *over Cairo—for seeing which, there is simply no substitute.*

Hey, listen, I didn't mean to tell you all this. I just meant to give you the bones of my report. But now I think about it, I guess it won't do any harm. I know I was sent out there to keep an eye on this crazy outing and to stop the guy getting into any really serious trouble, but I couldn't help making a few observations along the way. What I'm trying to say, Joey, is that we're really going to have to think about this stuff. Goodwill, I mean. Don't you realize, Joey? It's obvious. You can only really do goodwill if you are not only crazy but seen to be crazy. Forget the darkened limo, Joey. The guys in those things are perfectly sane. And guess what. Nobody ever believes a word they say, about goodwill or anything else. Trust me, Joey, nuttiness is the key to international stability. A guy rides up to the curbside after two and a half thousand miles thundering around the Egypt that no tourist ever sees, flying a

Sphinx. Go on, Joey, tell me. I positively challenge you. What the hell can you accuse him of? Waving with malice aforethought? Flying a balloon with intent? Having fun without a license?

Of course I'm not suggesting that we go right into this at the top. Naturally we'll need a little practice. But don't you think the Lincoln Memorial would look awful good flying over the Kremlin?

Now they can say they've seen it all—for the time being.

10

CHAPTER

The ELEPHANT Has Landed

Barry Coleman

A HOT AFTERNOON in Johore Bahru, Malaysia. Over in the girls' high school, the students are a trifle listless.

In the principal's office, where even the principal is beginning to flag (this is one of the hottest days of the summer), the phone rings. It's the King calling. (Or at least, the King's caller calling.) Listen, says the King's caller, His Majesty wants you to bring the girls right over to the golf course. The King says bring everybody.

Back at the country club, about halfway up the eighteenth, which is a fairly straightforward par-4, uphill, something is happening. For one thing, just short of halfway up, there stands an elephant. The golfers coming off the seventeenth regard the elephant with dismay. An ordinary elephant would be bad enough, standing just short of the length of a decent drive, but this one is much worse. It has a howdah. It is the height of a six-story building. Even if you lay up to it with, say, a five iron, it's still going to be very tricky to get over it and stay out of the trees.

And for another thing, the King is hurtling up and down the fairway on an enormous motorcycle.

Finally, as the girls' school crests the rise and begins to pour down the fairway, the golfers give up and make for the nineteenth, irritated. Just ahead of the students in their pale blue and white, there walks another, much smaller group in uniform, but these chaps are wearing red, emblazoned with gold. A couple of the redshirts walk up to the elephant and jump into a basket standing under its belly. There is a violent roaring noise. The elephant rises and begins to fly away.

So here's the King of Malaysia, deftly weaving between his subjects on his new Harley while a thousand schoolgirls line up on a golf course to take their turns for giggling rides in a flying elephant. An unlikely phenomenon sure enough, but one with a reasonably simple explanation. Indeed, the only conceivable expla-

nation. Malcolm Forbes is in Johore Bahru.

Last year I wrote a story about the Capitalist Tool campaign in Egypt. It was sort of a joke. What if, I asked—what if world leaders, who invariably glad-hand across the seas with promises of friendship and just as certainly travel around in darkened and bullet-proof limos—what if they took to visiting by motorcycle and flying wild balloons? Now, after the Tool trip to Asia, I'm not so sure it's funny. I mean, there really is something missing in these top-level encounters, vital as they are. And I know what it is. It's what we have when we go to Thailand, to Malaysia, to Singapore, and to Brunei and fly an elephant. It's fun.

I know world leaders can't have fun. But at the very least it's just as well someone comes along and has it for them. There is no known way of getting to know people better, quicker, than to fly a zany balloon over someone's town and land it in any available open space. By the time that elephant, that sphinx, is back in its bag, all the participants have formed impressions they won't forget in a long time.

We don't just meander aimlessly around these countries. We have a schedule—places to go, people to see. We travel in a sort of brisk cyclecade. No, more of a jumblecade. We have police vehicles out front, followed by the Tool riders (seven in this case), followed by a long tail of vans and trucks and ambulances and goodness-knows-what.

Anyhow, the jumblecade was just careering into Hua Hin when we met a very serious sleek black motorcade coming the other way. This was the cade of Mr. Wilfred Martens, the prime minister of Belgium, who had come to Thailand to talk about things like aluminum plants.

In a moment the Martenscade was a fast-diminishing black dot, on its way to do business. But the interesting thing was that for all the somber grandeur of the procession, Mr. Martens wasn't in it. His plane from Bangkok

Malcolm and sons Tim, Bob and Kip get a Buddhist blessing in Bangkok at the trip's beginning.

The schoolgirls and the elephant.

The King is inducted into the Capitalist Tools.

The King of Malaysia hurtling up and down the fairway.

Favorite pet.

The jumblecade keeps to schedule.

had been bounced by fog. If he had wanted to see the country, he should have come with us. If he had wanted to see the King (which I believe was his plan), likewise. We had dinner with the King and Queen in the garden of their summer palace that very evening. Really, going by motorcycle isn't all bad.

This was only the second time* that the Forbes Festival (that's what the Egyptians called it, and I think it's the best summation yet) had crossed national boundaries. In a way that probably means it's becoming more institutionalized, but don't worry. There are strict limits to the extent to which you can institutionalize a flying elephant and a string of Harley motorcycles.

But there were other changes, other advances. This year, for example, one of the

* The first: 1979, when Malcolm, son Bob, daughter Moira, and three cohorts first-timed it and motorcycled through Russia, entering via Germany, Czechoslovakia, and Poland.

cycles had a horn that played tunes. Not impressed? So what? All sorts of horns play tunes. Sure they do—a dozen notes in a single-line melody (of sorts); but this one played fifty tunes. It not only cheered us up on the highway and enabled us to offer the Doppler-effect versions of "Popeye," "Tiger Rag," and "God Bless America" to astonished passersby. It also had a highly ceremonial function. Its computer was loaded with the four appropriate national anthems.

The trip to Thailand was inspired partly by Her Majesty Queen Sirikit's visit to Forbes last year, and partly by the long and secure friendship between Thailand and the United States. There is, furthermore, probably no better time than the present to be reminding the Thais, in however indirect a fashion, of the general American awareness of their vital position in the superpower equation. Their eastern border is recognized across the democratic political spectrum as being of crucial significance as they are daily incursioned by the Vietnam occupiers of Cambodia.

Two years ago a witty columnist in Pakistan reminded us that all very well though balloons undoubtedly are, what his country really needed up in the air was F-16s. We of the Balloon Party leave the airplanes to the motorcades, but both Pakistan and Thailand are now in the F-16 club.

But visiting Thailand, it turns out, is a lot more than a well-wisher's visible expression. We were privileged to ride through one of the world's most fascinating, and rewarding, countries.

Another development this year was the expanded contingent of Forbeses. MSF, of course, plus Bob, Tim and Kip Forbes. Malcolm views his children as being, broadly speaking, one of two things: motorcyclists or "sensible." Bob and Tim have ridden many thousands of hot and dusty miles in the relentless tire tracks of their father; but sensible Kip joined us at the capitals on the itinerary, having organized great dinners in Bangkok, Kuala Lumpur and Singapore for their moguls of business and government.

Also on the road again were Denny Fleck, whose job it is to manage the considerable complexities of ballooning so far from home, and Kip Cleland, director of physical fitness, who scored a personal triumph this year in seeing his entire team effectively melted into shape by sun, humidity, and long hours on the road. Gerhard Heussler, German journalist, photographer, and super capitalist, was there to cover the cavalcade for the German media. Alain Guillou, famed French photographer, added fun to the run by projecting himself at dizzy angles through the windows of fast-moving vehicles while taking pictures.

Perhaps I should also mention that this year the festival enjoyed the considerable luxury of having its own transport to and from the event. The *Capitalist Tool* 727 made a complete circle around the globe in the course of taking the team to Bangkok via Tangier and Karachi and bringing them back from Brunei via Tokyo.

Our first official engagement in Bangkok was to fly the *Elephant* for Queen Sirikit. The day before, Malcolm had been interviewed by some young people who write and edit a paper called

We also do normal things, like touring the royal palace grounds.

I asked what the
graceful hand
movements
represented. "Just
gracefulness," she
said, "that's all."

Voice of the Children. He told them, with becoming modesty, that the Queen was coming to the launch. They were impressed, but asked, why isn't the King coming? Malcolm looked a bit taken aback. "Well, I don't quite know," he replied. "I guess he's busy, you know, being King."

Well, just hours before the launch, we did hear that the King wanted to come. Not only the King, but the two princesses, one the Crown Princess. It was a wonderful beginning to the trip. The thing about flying elephants and the strangely shaped hot air balloons in far lands is that there is always a certain uncertainty about how the country will take to it. People might not understand. Simple as the idea is, it is evidently sometimes hard to grasp. (Expatriate journalists seem to find it hardest. They just "know" there has to be more to it than MSF says there is. Nobody spends

hundreds of thousands of dollars of his own money swooping around the place on motorcycles, entertaining people, having fun, and being friendly. It isn't that kind of world.)

But the King and Queen seemed to understand it perfectly. While we waited for them to arrive at the Ampron Gardens, close to the Chitralada Palace, we in turn were entertained. A military band filled the gardens with the exotic modulations of Thai music, and groups of traditional performers and dancers performed a series of most expressive exhibitions.

In a way, the dancers and the elephant were a perfect cultural exchange: both speak, wordlessly, for themselves. I asked once what the exquisitely graceful hand movements of Thai dancing represented. My informant looked puzzled for a second and then smiled that irrepressible Thai smile. "Just gracefulness," she said—"that's all." I should have known. We

have heard this rather useful Oriental message before, in other terms. The medium is the message. Thereafter I accepted the richness of the costumes, the sweet urgency of the music, and the eloquence of the dancing in the spirit in which they were intended. And whenever I was asked the why of elephant and motorcycles, I said, "Just friendliness—that's all."

The first flight of the *Great Sky Elephant*, tethered though it was, was a great success. In the background rose the extravagantly gilded gables of palaces and temples; in the foreground, in front of a huge crowd, two real elephants, dwarfed, took a couple of well-chosen steps backward. It wasn't a perfectly calm evening, so the *Sky Elephant* flapped a little, shaking a leg and waggling its ears.

The royal princesses, however, were not deterred. To our delight, they both took a ride and loved it. But Princess Nanachakri Sirindhorn wasn't entirely satisfied. "Is that it?" she asked Malcolm. "Won't it go any higher? I want to go higher!" A tough corner for MSF. On the one hand, in fables a crown princess has only to wish . . . on the other, the King wants the princess home in one piece. Happily, this princess was willing to wait for a less wildly windy day.

The following morning the *Great Sky Elephant* took its first free flight. It's easy to be flippant about the notion of a gigantic elephant flying over Bangkok. But thrilling though it is, it's also quite an inspiring sight. I don't quite know why. Perhaps it's less the elephant than the combination of circumstances that brought it about, the million-to-one chance that an individual who had the wish, the urge, the nerve to do it, would also have the financial and logistical capability. Fortunately, not only those of us who were there that morning will have the pleasure of watching the event; a two-unit film crew

The Elephant Has Landed · 251

The balloon is blessed while (BELOW) the official T-shirt is presented to the royal family.

Riding the real thing for once.

The Elephant Has Landed · 253

(OPPOSITE) Crown Princess Nanachakri Sirindhorn aloft in a heavy wind.

The old and the new in Ayutthaya.

was also there. All being well, the Asia trip will become, like China and Egypt, a television special.

No sooner was the elephant back in the bag than we were on the road. The road, frankly, took us by surprise. It was hot out there. Really hot. By the time we reached our first destination, a couple of hundred miles north of Bangkok, we were desperate. We had had a couple of gas stops, and we had each drunk a couple of gallons of chilled soda water. Even so, we all felt at least fifteen pounds lighter. Survive this, we all thought, and we'll be ready for anything.

That's one thing about a Forbes expedition that isn't immediately obvious. Seen in the lobby of the Oriental Hotel in Bangkok, the Regent in Kuala Lumpur or the Shangri-La in Singapore, caught off guard in the adequately appointed fuselage of the *Capitalist Tool*, the team would appear to be having a reasonably comfortable time of it. And that, certainly, would be true. On the other hand, nine hours into a journey on a rumbling, shaking motorcycle that began with a five o'clock call and featured 120-degree temperatures, 80 percent humidity, and two balloon launches immediately after what would have been breakfast if you had time for any, it looks slightly different.

This is hardly a complaint: we go for the motorcycling and the ballooning, not for the hotel laundry service; but it's a point. Secretly, these trips are hard work. There's an element of boot camp to them that we suspect may not be entirely incidental. After a couple of days in the heat and humidity of Bangkok, Kip Forbes was convinced that MSF, in particular, had met his

meteorological match. He'd never make it. We'd end up flying home.

Two weeks later, when we thundered into Singapore, the beam on Malcolm's face as he sprung out of the saddle said otherwise. I didn't understand it until the dinner Forbes gave in Singapore for representative members of the local community. Malcolm chose to speak about ingenious and energetic developments in the American economy. In passing he mentioned the application of technology to medicine. Oliver Wendell Holmes, he pointed out, had predicted that one day we would not die of disease, we would simply wear out. But not yet, apparently.

We flew in Korat and then rolled all the way back through Bangkok to Pattaya, the chief among Thailand's new beach resorts. Thailand has beautiful beaches, no question of that, and a gift for hospitality that translates into delightful and highly effective service in restaurants and hotels throughout the land. Pattaya initially developed as an R&R refuge during the war, and no wonder. Now it is part of a more conventional tourism development, but it somehow re-

After the flight in Korat the packed-up balloon was carried out by one fellow—a feat that awed our fitness director.

It was hot so icy receptions were welcome.

On the road again.

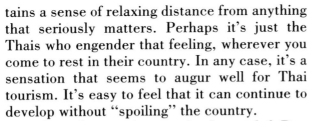

Young Thai Buddhists become monks for three months, a spiritual training they say is never forgotten.

Gracefulness on a beach in Pattaya.

tains a sense of relaxing distance from anything that seriously matters. Perhaps it's just the Thais who engender that feeling, wherever you come to rest in their country. In any case, it's a sensation that seems to augur well for Thai tourism. It's easy to feel that it can continue to develop without "spoiling" the country.

Early in the morning, on the day we left Pattaya, we were scheduled to fly the *Elephant* again. As it happened, it was too windy, so, a mite disappointed, we flew the conventional backup balloon. We were taken out to a large sandy space close to the local wat, the Buddhist temple. The preparations were splendid. Under a small pavilion, chairs were arranged from which we could enjoy more traditional dancing, but not before the monks, serious that morning against the ever-cheerful orange of their robes, had filed past to accept donations in their wooden bowls.

Buddhism dominates Thailand and the Thai approach to the world, but not as other religious disciplines have occasionally dominated elsewhere. It is a much more subtle, more infusive kind of influence, which one senses as contributing simultaneously to both the gentleness and the extraordinary toughness of the Thai people. The monks have, literally, nothing but their bowls. A society in which it is common for most young men, at some time, to become monks cannot ever become obsessively acquisitive. Whatever happens in Thailand, it will remain, for us, forever exotic.

256

Under the pavilion a small uniformed band played a colorful and highly determined version of "The Stars and Stripes Forever" while the balloon was made ready, and we, ever anxious to reciprocate, played the Thai national anthem. On our motorcycle, of course.

Harley-Davidsons have frequently been described as powerful; but there is no motorcycle so powerful in Thailand as one that plays the Thai national anthem. For a moment, the band and the onlookers were nonplused. It wasn't immediately obvious where the sound was coming from. After all, it couldn't be from that large red motorcycle. . . .

When they realized, some seconds after they were already standing at attention, that there really was no alternative, some of the band felt moved to salute. There was nowhere else to face, so everyone faced the Harley—including us. Another memorable scene.

This water buffalo did not like being roused from his mud bath.

By midafternoon we were in Hua Hin. Hearing that we were in town, King Bhumiphol Adulydej invited us to dinner at the palace. As I look back on it, it seems dreamlike. That's not surprising. It seemed dreamlike at the time.

Dinner—a vast barbecue, if that's not too vulgar a word—was delicately distributed beneath the tall palms on the palace lawn. Lanterns hung shimmering on the breeze, and out to sea a navy training vessel was outlined in what looked from that distance like white fairy lights. In a salon open to the lawn an orchestra was assembled. Navy personnel, they were dressed in whites, and they played enchanting music. It sounded Thai, but it was still more redolent of a kind of American big-band Forties sound. More surprising, more interesting yet, was that some of the songs they played, sung by a blissful lineup of white-uniformed ladies of the sea, had been composed by the King. Lovely songs, too, very touching. I was told they were love songs. The King not only composes; he plays. Fridays he gets together with the band, and Saturdays anything good they

An enterprising youth figures balloons should move.

The Navy band in Pattaya played "The Stars and Stripes Forever"; our melodic Harley returned the salute.

A detour to Hua Hin brought an unscheduled high-light—dinner with the royal family at their summer palace.

have come up with is played on the radio, the King on sax or maybe clarinet. On really big occasions, when visiting jazz giants are in town, the King invites them over to the palace to jam. Thailand is a surprising and, indeed, enchanted country.

South of Hua Hin, the countryside also began to take on a more ethereal look. We wound through hill and jungle on our way to the other coast, on the Andaman Sea, at Phuket. South of Phuket, a couple of days later, we began to run between those strangely abrupt towers of rock, usually whiskery with every kind of vegetation, which characterize the Far Eastern landscapes of our childhood. No landscape could look like that, not in real life, but this one does. Off Phuket, those towers rise out of warm and misty seas, full of pearls.

We flew the *Elephant* in Phuket, and again in Songkhla, near Hat Yai, before we rode away from Thailand to make our first border crossing. As we rode up to the border, we all must have realized pretty much at once what a border would mean to the festival, as to anyone else: comparisons.

Some of the contrasts were anticipated. In riding to Malaysia, we would ride from an officially Buddhist to an officially Muslim state, from a realm that had somehow resisted imperialists through the ages to a former colony of the British. We would ride from a culture in which even the alphabet is incomprehensible to one in which the phonetic use of the Roman alphabet would in some ways seem all too familiar (we would go *ekspress* to the *feri*, our balloons following in a *lori*). Comparisons never seem quite fair. More useful to a festival crew are the features the cultures have in common.

We get to find out a lot about a country by flying an elephant, or a sphinx. Mainly that's because it's completely unrehearsable. We make our preparations to get the thing into the air, but that's all. What happens then has to do first with the wind, and then with the nature of the people who witness the landing. What we found in Malaysia, as we had found in Thailand, was a ready sense of humor and a terrific friendliness. The people knew we were offbeat —anyone could see that—but it was obviously a harmless, indeed friendly, craziness, and the Malaysians repaid it in kind. That's what hot air elephanteering is all about.

Malaysia, of course, is regarded as Southeast Asia's economic miracle. It strikes one at first as a fairly prosperous, fairly snappy sort of place, and there is evidence of lively economic activity both in resorts like Penang and in old-established tin-mining towns like Ipoh. But it isn't until you get to the astonishing city of Kuala Lumpur that you realize what's going on in Malaysia. A few years ago, KL was a backwater to Singapore, slowly capturing space from the jungle. Today it looks like Houston, only faster. Rubber and tin are the staples upon which this economic outburst is based, but the impetus now seems to come from such newcomers as high-technology processes and services like insurance, transport, real estate, and accommodation. And inevitably, the Malaysians are just like the rest of us. There's been a slowdown recently, and they don't much care for it. Some grumbling is to be heard in the land.

In any case, Malaysia isn't all boom. Across a demographic spectrum that features three main communities, Malay, Chinese, and Indian, there is still an unmistakable whiff of Britishness. You are bound to notice it when, after ten days straight of the exotic and unpronounceable, you roll through a town called Butterworth.

Kip Cleland and I noticed it in another interesting way. We had an afternoon off in KL, so we figured we would play golf; we had heard there were some pretty good courses there. And that is true enough. But try getting a game on one. Exclusivity on a truly colonial scale is now the rule in Boom City, so don't take your clubs. Not even a call to the Prime Minister's office could get us a game without our playing with a member. Finally, we were introduced to a member and we went over to the clubhouse, a new building of epic proportions, which had somehow contrived the uniquely musty smell of a British officers' mess. Amazing. The only explanation must be an aerosol, perhaps called Clubmustiness, produced in KL by yet another enterprising Malaysian.

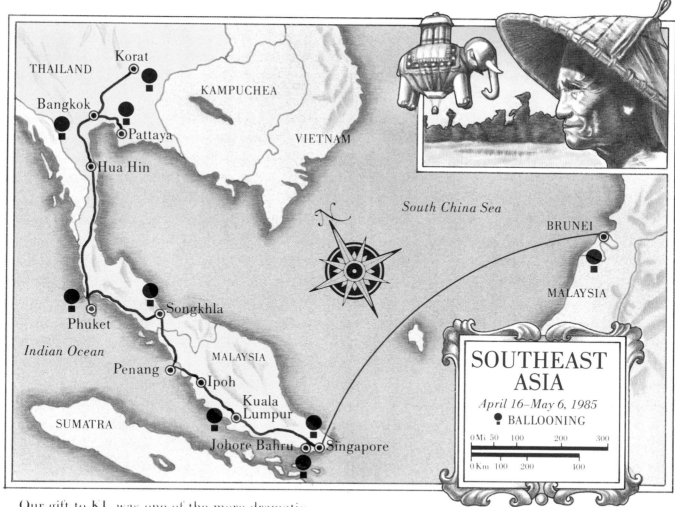

KORAT
THAILAND
Bangkok
Pattaya
Hua Hin
KAMPUCHEA
VIETNAM
South China Sea
BRUNEI
MALAYSIA
Phuket
Indian Ocean
Songkhla
MALAYSIA
Penang
Ipoh
Kuala Lumpur
SUMATRA
Johore Bahru
Singapore

SOUTHEAST ASIA
April 16–May 6, 1985
● BALLOONING
0 Mi 50   100   200   300
0 Km 100   200   400

Our gift to KL was one of the more dramatic festival flights. Launching from the cricket ground (where else), Malcolm took aloft none other than the Prime Minister himself, Datuk Seri Dr. Mathir Mohamed—the festival's first ever. The flight was short, what with the PM being a busy man; and challenging, there being some shortage of suitable landing areas. It's always quite a business, from the bureaucratic point of view, this landing. It doesn't seem bureaucratically sensible to fly a device over whose direction you have absolutely no control. Time and again they ask us if we would like to tour the area to review possible landing sites. We explain that it isn't really necessary because . . . well, because . . . you see, we can't really control . . . but we don't press it too hard, because if they did catch on, they might not let us loose. Again, you could hardly blame them.

In Songkhla, the Governor of the province and the Governor of the Tourism Authority of Thailand get taken for a ride.

Getting ready at Kuala Lumpur's famed cricket club. Passenger for the free flight: the Prime Minister.

So there was Malcolm, three or four hundred feet up with the Prime Minister and nowhere to put him down. Another tricky spot. In the end they spotted a promising-looking piece of grass about half the size of the balloon. It happened to be the grass-and-garden bank of a major highway. The instant the basket hit, the PM was rushed away by his apoplectic security men. In interviews with the press, Malcolm praised the Prime Minister's courage; it was probably all that stood between him and a stiff jail sentence.

In each capital the press asked, "Why?" "Just friendliness, that's all" was the reply.

All this was in the papers when we rode down next day to call in on the King of Malaysia at Johore Bahru. The King, Mahmood Iskander Ibni Al-Marhum Sultan Ismail, had obviously read about the PM's flight. He has his differences with the Prime Minister, and he wasn't particularly thrilled at the idea of the PM getting such a play for his display of high-flown courage. The king of Malaysia may change almost as often as the prime minister, if not more so, since the job rotates among the country's nine sultans on a five-year basis. This seems to give them a pretty equal footing when it comes to a wrangle, and Dr. Mathir Mohamed has found this king to be a colorful sparring partner.

When we got to the appointed meeting place, the golf course, the King was still out polishing off nine holes. As we heard it, he wins a lot. When he came in, he was plainly riveted by the Harleys. Indeed, he expressed such earnest and unstinted admiration that Malcolm was moved to give him one. The King was ecstatic, as who wouldn't be. "Only last week," he said, "I wrote to our consul general in New York asking for brochures of the whole Harley range. I have wanted a Harley for such a long time. And now, God has sent me one." I thought for a moment Malcolm was lost for words. "Well, er, small 'g,' Your Majesty," he said.

And so it was that he rode up and down on his Harley while the *Elephant* entertained the school. He didn't take a ride in the balloon,

Wedging through Kuala Lumpur traffic. A few years ago it was a backwater to Singapore. Today it looks like Houston, only faster.

note. That was left to his baby grandson, to the schoolgirls . . . and the prime minister.

We rode over the causeway to Singapore an hour later. Singapore is a city whose claims to cleanliness, greenness, lawfulness, and low-cost electronics are more than justified. It is also quite possibly the most futuristic town in the world. The new buildings, mostly tall, are usually handsome and frequently downright glamorous. Yet there is something unnerving about Singapore. Nobody likes dirt or crime, but the ways in which you get rid of them may matter more than we think. Someone said that Singapore was a fine city. Fine you for almost everything. It is also a capital city. Hang you not only for murder but for rape and drug dealing. That will suit some people; others may find it disturbing. Whatever, it is undoubtedly the case that Singapore is changing, and the somewhat autocratic rule it has known for many years is now subject to fiercer questioning than ever before.

We flew the *Elephant* in Singapore, and although the press took to it with great enthusiasm, it wasn't, truth to tell, much of a public occasion. Singapore was terribly busy that morning. It's terribly busy every morning.

The trip ended in a rather reflective mood. It also ended in Brunei, a place which, if nothing else, will give rise to any amount of reflection. Brunei is a small state on the northern margin of the large island that is mainly composed of Borneo and Sarawak. The Sultan of Brunei is said now to be the richest man in the world. The source of his wealth is oil. Simple as that.

The Sultan is also distinguished as the owner of the largest private residential building in the

In the basket: Singapore eyewitness news report.

world, his palace. His subjects now enjoy one of the highest per capita incomes in the world. Brunei may soon have more entries in the *Guinness Book of World Records* than any other country.

The Brunei international airport might merit an entry on its own. Something to do with the ratio of traffic to size of terminal buildings. It already has a spread of large and modern buildings (eerily deserted when we arrived) which is currently being doubled in size. As we understand it, there are currently two flights a week to Brunei. And since the population is in the

The Elephant Has Landed · 261

region of 200,000, it is unlikely that the demand will rise much whatever the size of the terminal buildings. Brunei is a state in which none of the normal rules of economics seem to apply. And yet my feeling is, they get you in the end.

The citizens of Brunei are paid by the state just for being there. The current rate is said to be the equivalent of $15,000 per annum. Now this in itself may produce some interesting results. We flew the balloon (with the enthusiastic cooperation of the authorities). The Sultan himself didn't show up but sent the 19-year-old Crown Prince. There was a large crowd, on the nice new ceremonial field next to the new mosque (the largest new mosque in Asia, or some such record). I have mentioned before that the landing of the balloon tells us a lot about a nation. Brunei was the only place we have ever flown where people who arrived at the landing flat refused to help us roll up the balloon and put it away. Interesting. Not conclusive, but interesting. Finally a few people did help us anyway, with the same good-natured friendliness we have been privileged to meet everywhere.

Another year—the Year of the *Elephant*. We met a lot of people and had a lot of fun. Ever since Pakistan we have enjoyed the multiple benefits of a team song. We borrowed it from Willie Nelson, and those of us who were there will never forget, for example, Colonel Mohamed Akram singing it to us 15,000 feet up on the Karakoram Highway to keep our spirits up. This year, of course, we had it on the horn, and Denny played it every time we set off at the crack of dawn and every time we pulled away from a gas station. It's true, it keeps our spirits up. Not only that, but it explains, at least to us, the simple reason we do this stuff.

On the road again,
Goin' places that I've never been.
Seein' things that I may never see again,
And I can't wait to get on the road again.

As the sun sinks slowly in the west, the scene becomes a painter's dream. Thailand combines a breathtaking spectrum of colorful skies and sunsets with miles of beaches—an exotic paradise.

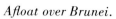
Afloat over Brunei.

UPS AND DOWNS

Malcolm Forbes

For many happy years we've been taking off a few days every summer from FORBES' Trinchera Ranch at Fort Garland, Colorado, to motorcycle through a different chunk of the country. Even after an occasional day of burst skies, hailstones or gale winds, we hardly ever have ended some hours of riding without awe-filled observations about America the Beautiful.

Except one July day in 1984.

It was not because the land was less stunning, but because, at some speed (legal, doubtless), I came off the motorcycle and came to, stunned. So that summer's safari ended in seeing a very different segment of the country —as uplifting, eye-opening, surprising, wondrous as anything on our previous trips.

* * *

Doctors know all about reaction to shock, but you and I don't until we've had it. A little while after regaining awareness as to why we were where we were at the side of the road, I suggested we get back on the bikes and push on to our destination 70 miles up and over Glacier National Park's Going-to-the-Sun Highway.

The other three bikers—Norwegian doctor Jan Engzelius, a St. Mark's classmate of son Tim; FORBES Trinchera Ranch Manager Errol Ryland; and Chattanooga nephew Jamie Hudlow—gave me the kind of look that you and I gave our kids when they wanted their fourth hot dog, fifth ice cream cone and a first ride on the roller coaster when it was long past time to go home. Dripping baby-talk-tone patience, they explained it was time to go elsewhere.

In that breathtaking part of western Montana bordering Canada, people and towns are so far spread out that a hospital must serve a vast area to do its thing. Fortunately, the nearest hospital I was hauled to had a helicopter medical unit to dip into the hidden crevices that snag hikers, skim over lakes that sometimes lacerate water sporters and, of course, pick up the inevitable roadside wrecked.

A while later I was in the emergency room of Kalispell Regional Hospital being speared through the chest with a tube to a collapsed lung, having broken ribs counted and all sorts of wires attached to print out whether the concussion was likely to recur or was merely a

Sure motorcycling has risks, such as a patch of loose gravel in Montana's Glacier National Park which resulted in three broken ribs, a collapsed lung, a concussion and a bevy of abrasions. Ten days later, feeling almost whole again, I felt up to a balloon ride . . .

264

chronic condition (as is so often contended by some FORBES readers). "Abrasions" was the word used to cover what developed into superb rivals for Turner-like impressionisms.

There were some hours of the days and nights when I felt I had already become a live-in buddy of the guy who carries the three-pronged pitchfork. I knew damned (correct usage) well where the Sting of the fellow with the Reaper was. My interest was in discovering where that "peace at the end" bit had gone.

Gradually, more frequent hours of feeling good were so good it's hard to exaggerate how good. The mind boggles how, in pain, one's sense of proportion gets turned topsy-turvy—like looking at a star through the wrong end of the telescope at the Palomar Observatory.

Gratitude for a Guggenheim Fellowship or a Pulitzer Prize couldn't come close to equaling the overwhelming appreciation one feels when a nurse hands you a wee speck of something and says, "This will make you feel better."

It may be a crazy world, but it's never crazy enough to let any of us long stay unreminded of our own momentariness, unreminded that you can't live life with no sense of proportion, no sense of limitation.

* * *

It's really soul-lifting how helpful people want to be when they have the opportunity to be. In that hospital and among that staff one saw another dimension, a deeper one, really, of America the Beautiful.

The Down of this motorcycle trip provided perhaps more Up than any of the others.

But, thank you, once is enough.

Running Out of Hot Air Is

something you never do in our business if you want to stay in it.

In the sport of ballooning, the same can be said.

You can see what happens if you do.

On its heralded maiden flight in the U.S., our great golden *Sphinx II*, built for and flown all over Egypt on our friendship salute, was participating in New Jersey's major balloon festival. At 2,400 feet the top panel of the center, containing heat that lifts the balloon, inexplicably popped. The *Sphinx* caved in, and our precipitous drop was instantly under way.

We were saved from lasting disaster by that wondrous critter's cold-air-filled appendages—the forepaws, head and tail. In previous flights in the Land of the Nile and in France, we'd griped at the length of time it took to deflate those parts after the swift venting of the hot-air-filled middle. Our attitude, as we rapidly lost altitude, changed at the same rate.

The *Sphinx*, now undergoing postmortem and repair, will rise again and, thanks to its head, tail and paws, so will we.

The first hot-air-balloon flight in Fiji and the maiden voyage of the newest Capitalist Tool balloon. Because Fiji is a nation of 322 islands, there's water everywhere, so to speak, and so it involved a bit of moral and physical courage on the part of the Governor General of Fiji, Ratu Sir Penaia Ganilau, to be the passenger.

Afterword

EVERYTHING'S "DANGEROUS." Living is dangerous. Eventually everybody dies of it—so far.

Sure, motorcycling has risks. If you hit, heavier hurts are more likely than when you are sealed off in a car. On the other hand, you know that, so all your senses are more alert. People go to sleep in cars, but almost never on motorcycles.

Sure, ballooning can be dangerous. But it looks infinitely more so than it is. Balloon accidents, with rare exceptions, are the result of pilot carelessness. In terms of flights and hours and numbers, fatalities are minimal.

But it is a fact that in both these ways of going, I've gone down unintentionally—to which these pictures bear witness.

Because such occasional splats are so visible, don't be deterred from trying either, or moving out by any other means that appeals. Walk. Hike. Jog. Swim. Ski. Dive. Soar. Fly. Drive. Pedal. Hitch. Sail. No matter what, somebody's been hurt (or worse) doing any of 'em.

Always keep in mind that the highest accident rate is in the home, especially getting in and out of the bathtub. Crossing the street's very dangerous. And what's left to eat that hasn't at one time or another been accused of causing cancer? Or where's the air that hasn't been condemned for some contaminant or other, natural (bee droppings) or "man-made" (dust, rapidly marching deserts), as well as innumerable other pollutions?

Staying in bed is probably the most dangerous of all. Bedsores, pneumonia, and all that. Nowadays, even after the most searching surgery, it's on your feet within hours to avoid the complications of too long beddy-bye.

In spite of all this we're living ever longer. (So many of us will be older longer that there's a question of whether we—or our children— can afford it.)

So venture out.

Adventure.

You'll live longer if your spirit's stirred by the world about you, be it the next village, the next border, the next continent, or the next planet. The worst hurt to mind and life is never to have moved out at all. That's really crippling.

Don't be a shut-in when there's America the Beautiful to see from sea to shining sea. Don't stay put when you can put foot into any part of this still whole, wide, and mostly wonderful world.

—Malcolm Forbes

271

PHOTO CREDITS

Illustrations

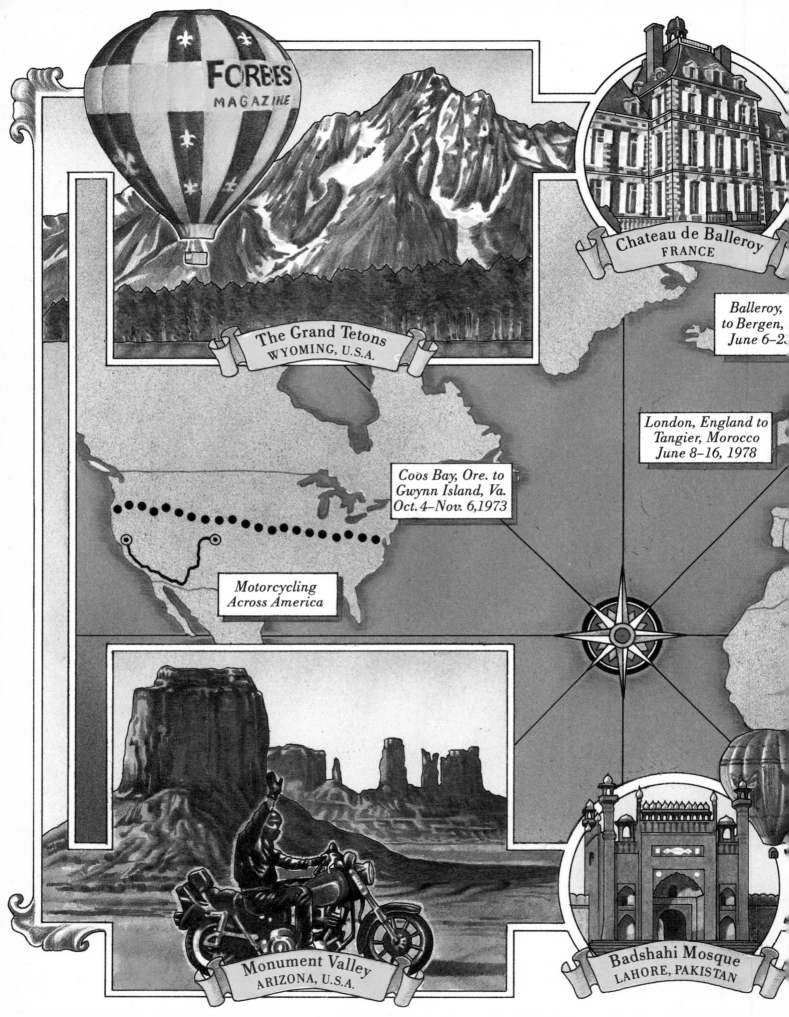

FORBES MAGAZINE

The Grand Tetons
WYOMING, U.S.A.

Chateau de Balleroy
FRANCE

Balleroy,
to Bergen,
June 6–2.

London, England to
Tangier, Morocco
June 8–16, 1978

Coos Bay, Ore. to
Gwynn Island, Va.
Oct. 4–Nov. 6, 1973

Motorcycling
Across America

Monument Valley
ARIZONA, U.S.A.

Badshahi Mosque
LAHORE, PAKISTAN